solutions at work

practical guides to managing disability

employers' forum on disability

solutions at work

practical guides to managing disability

Sponsored by

UNUMPROVIDENT

Solutions at work – practical guides to managing disability

Published by the Employers' Forum on Disability 2002.

Design: Jewell Design, Hove.
Print: Hubbard Print, Sheffield.

Editor-in-chief: Susan Scott-Parker
Publishing Manager: Ed Myllès

ISBN 1-903894-03-4

Additional copies are available from:

Publications Department
Employers' Forum on Disability
Nutmeg House
60 Gainsford Street
London SE1 2NY

www.employers-forum.co.uk

The Forum would like to thank Philip Dowdle, Paul Drake, Caroline Gooding, Bela Gor, Catherine Hammond, Richard Southorn and all of our Associates for their contribution to the series of Briefing Papers.

The Forum is grateful to Cornell University's New York State School of Industrial and Labor Relations for providing a model for the series of Briefing Papers.

This publication is available in other formats.

Contents

Commitment and ability are critical

The Disability Discrimination Act (1995) demonstrates a positive commitment by the government to change the futures of disabled people in the UK. There is also growing understanding amongst employers that the DDA requires them to make adjustments, where reasonable, in order that disabled people can continue to contribute to the business.

At UnumProvident we, as employers, set out to make adjustments. What needs to be done is usually easily managed and not nearly as costly as we had originally anticipated (indeed, the average cost of adjustments across the business community is now estimated at around £200). We are delighted to be sponsoring the publication of this compendium of best practice advice in how to make adjustments for people with disabilities at work in a way which focuses on practical manageable business solutions. When you consider that sickness absence can cost up to 16% of payroll it quickly becomes apparent that a commitment and ability to retain staff who become disabled should be a critical part of business planning.

By sponsoring this book as well as the Forum series of Briefing Papers on which it is based, we hope to encourage organisations to understand that being disability confident makes sound business sense.

Susan Ring,
Chairman and Managing Director
UnumProvident

The Forum – Making it easier

Our job at the Forum is to make it easier for our members and other employers to recruit, retain and develop disabled employees. The business case is compelling:

- managing a diverse workforce is increasingly recognised as a key factor in improving efficiency, productivity and overall business success
- there are over 8.7 million disabled adults in the UK alone, making up a large and growing proportion of employees, existing and potential customers and stakeholders and, indeed, shareholders
- in addition, by the year 2010, 40 per cent of the UK labour force will be 45 or over, the age at which disability begins to increase significantly

Our aim is to help create organisations in which everyone is enabled to channel their skills, experience and energy towards business success.

There is now legislation in place to protect disabled people in the UK and, of course, we need to understand what the Disability Discrimination Act (1995) says. Even more important, though, is that our managers and colleagues understand what this legislation truly means.

In our experience, organisations acknowledging the need to become truly disability confident have much to learn. Positive policies on disability are not enough. They must be matched by investment in the in-house expertise required to move quickly to practical solutions when someone's mental or physical impairment begins to have an adverse affect on their performance at work.

In fact, our biggest challenge is to adjust the way we think. If we can ensure colleagues no longer make assumptions regarding what people can do – assumptions based solely on a disability label – we will have gone a long way towards creating a culture which truly embraces diversity in its widest sense. The adjustments described in this book – to policies and to working practices – will make it easier for everyone to contribute to business success.

It is hugely liberating when people immediately connect the word 'disability' to the assumption "what adjustments would enable the person to do the job". The case studies in this book show the benefits to Forum members on the road to becoming disability confident.

S Scott Parker

Susan Scott-Parker,
Chief Executive,
Employers' Forum on Disability

Solutions at work – introduction

This book presents fifteen years of know-how, developed 'at the coal face' working closely with members of the Employers' Forum on Disability. Our job is to make it easier for employers to benefit from the contribution of disabled people to business success. Our message is simple: mere compliance with the law is not enough: it is only when we work to the spirit of the new legislation that both employers and disabled people benefit.

The Forum was established by the business community because of the compelling business case for positioning disability as a diversity, equal opportunities, employment, customer care and marketing priority. However, people can find it difficult to approach disability in a business-like way; many hold dated, negative views due to lack of personal experience and information.

People can find it difficult to change their way of looking at disability because the term covers such a wide range of very different people. Many do not see disabled people as individuals and focus exclusively on their impairments or diagnoses, in effect, defining people solely by their disabilities. For example, an accountant who develops epilepsy becomes 'an epileptic' – her accountancy skills are disregarded.

What we deal with in this book is the necessary understanding of the technical solutions that can now empower disabled people in the workplace. All to often people feel uneasy by their lack of experience and overwhelmed because they do not know what to do or where to start. Consequently, good people are lost to the organisation.

This book will help you ensure a co-ordinated efficient response when an applicant or employee requires an adjustment due to their disability. The case studies show that all types of organisations can, and do, make adjustments that benefit employees minimising sickness absence and the costs related to redundancy and starting the recruitment process anew. There is compelling evidence that organisations skilled in making adjustments are more responsive to the potential contribution of every employee. It is worth noting that the average cost of adjustments is now estimated at circa £200.

It is important to understand that the responsibility (and ability) for saying "yes, we will make this adjustment" rests as close to the frontline as possible. Responsibility, then, for saying "no, we regard this adjustment as unreasonable" should be placed higher in the organisation because:

1. **Senior management get an overview which reveals that too many reasonable adjustments are being refused which – then triggers investigation.**

2. The obligation to justify to senior management a refusal to make an adjustment will in itself encourage a positive approach.

The Forum believes that, to change attitudes and behaviour, organisational policies and personal contact with disabled people must occur in tandem. The Forum recommends:

- **involving disabled employees in process and policy development**
- **disabled expert advisers joining senior executives at briefings, dinners and consultations**
- **commissioning disabled trainers and consultants to increase employees knowledge, confidence and skills at the interpersonal level**
- **providing work experience to disabled job seekers**
- **investing in consultation with and career development of disabled employees**

The essence of this book will enable you as a manager to enable your workforce to meet the needs of your business.

employers' forum on disability

When training and developing supervisor/ management skills, this book should be used in conjunction with two other Forum publications:

Unlocking Potential – the new disability business case, and

Promoting Change – becoming a disability confident organisation

(see pages 184/5 for summaries of Forum publications).

employers' forum on disability

Sponsored by

UNUMPROVIDENT

Chapter One

Management Solutions

A BRIEF INTRODUCTION TO

The Disability Discrimination Act (DDA) 1995

- What the Act does
- Who is affected by the Act
- Goods, facilities, services and property
- How do we know what the DDA means?

1.1

What the Act does

The Act gives disabled people the right not to be discriminated against in the areas of employment, getting goods and services, and buying or renting land or property. The Act requires schools, colleges and universities to provide information for disabled people.

The Act allows the Government to set minimum standards so that disabled people can use public transport more easily.

The Disability Rights Commission was launched in April 2000. As well as its advisory and educative role the Commission has enforcement powers to enable it to fulfil its task of securing civil rights for disabled people. These powers include:

- **power to conduct formal investigations**
- **power to serve non-discrimination notices**
- **power to act over persistent discrimination**
- **power to provide assistance to an individual who is bringing proceedings in connection with unlawful discrimination**
- **power to issue Codes of Practice**
- **power for conciliation of disputes**

In Northern Ireland the equivalent body is the Equality Commission of Northern Ireland.

Who is affected by the act

Disabled people

The Act gives rights to disabled people who have or have had a disability which makes it difficult for them to carry out normal day-to-day activities. The disability could be physical, sensory or mental. It must also be substantial and have a long-term effect, i.e. it must last or be expected to last for 12 months. Progressive conditions, which have a slight effect on day-to-day activities, but are expected to become substantial, are covered as are conditions which have a substantial effect for short periods but are likely to recur. Severe disfigurement is also classed as a disability.

1.1

Employers and service providers

Employers and people who provide goods and services to the public have to ensure that they are not discriminating against disabled people. Many of course have to take measures both as an employer and as someone who provides goods and services to the public. In some instances, this may require employers and service providers making reasonable adjustments to the way in which their services are run or employment organised (termed "reasonable adjustments" by the DDA).

Landlords or others who are responsible for letting or selling property

People who sell or let property have to ensure that they do not discriminate against people.

The rights for disabled people

Employment

It is unlawful for an employer to treat a disabled person less favourably than someone else for a reason related to their disability, unless there is a "material and substantial reason".

This means decisions must not be based on stereotypical assumptions, and that if employers have any concerns they must make proper investigations.

The DDA requires more than treating everyone the same, because in some cases this might disadvantage a disabled person. In these situations, employers must ask themselves if they can show a substantial reason for such an action.

In addition, employers have a duty to make any reasonable adjustments to the workplace, or to the way work is done, which would ensure that a disabled employee or applicant is not substantially disadvantaged.

The DDA applies to all employment matters including recruitment, training, performance management, protection from harassment, promotion and dismissal.

The employment part of the Act does not apply to employers who employ fewer than 15 people, though they will be encouraged to follow good practice guidelines. This exclusion of small employers will be removed in 2004 when the DDA will apply to all employers regardless of size. It also does not currently apply to operational staff employed in the armed forces, the police, the prison services, or to anyone employed on board ships, hovercrafts or aeroplanes. The Government proposes, however, to extend the DDA to cover all of the above except the armed forces.

The Quota Scheme

Registration (known as the 'Green Card') and the Quota Scheme ended with the introduction of the DDA. With the new employment rights under the DDA, disabled people no longer need to register and employers are no longer required to employ a quota of registered disabled people.

Goods, facilities, services and property

The Act prohibits disability discrimination by anyone who provides goods, facilities or services to members of the public whether paid for or free. This could range from selling bread in a supermarket, using the facilities in a launderette, to borrowing a book from a public library. A 'service that consists of the use of a means of transport', that is to say a vehicle, is excluded from Part 3. Transport buildings and infrastructure, and services provided within them are however covered by Part 3 in the same way as other buildings are. Private clubs are also excluded.

It is against the law to treat a disabled person less favourably for a reason related to their disability, without legal justification by:

- **refusing to serve. For example, if a supermarket owner refuses to serve someone whose disability means that they shop slowly**
- **providing a worse standard of service. For example, if a restaurant owner insists that a person with a facial disfigurement sits out of sight of the other customers**
- **providing a service to a disabled person on worse terms. For example, asking a disabled person for a bigger deposit when they are booking a holiday simply because of their disability**

Legal justifications for less favourable treatment

It is not against the law to refuse to treat a disabled person less favourably or differently because of their disability if:

- **the health and safety of the disabled person or other people would be endangered**
- **the disabled person cannot give informed consent or agree to the terms of the service because of their disability**

- **the service provider would otherwise be unable to serve the disabled customers, or other members of the public**

- **any extra charge for a service reflects the greater cost of providing that service because of the person's disability (however, the service provider cannot charge a disabled customer more to cover the cost of complying with their legal duty to make their service accessible)**

1.1 **Service providers must also change the way goods, facilities and services are provided.**

Service providers must make reasonable adjustments to the way in which their services are provided if disabled customers find it unreasonably difficult or impossible to use their services.

Specifically providers must consider:

- **providing equipment or other helpful items which make it easier for disabled people to use their service, if it is reasonable to do so. For example, an induction loop might make it easier for people who use hearing aids**

- **changing any policies or practices which make it impossible or unreasonably difficult for disabled people to use the service. For example, accepting complaints over the telephone where an individual is unable because of their disability to comply with a policy requiring all complaints to be in writing**

- **providing other ways of letting disabled people use their services, if it is reasonable to do so. For example, if a library's reference section is on the first floor, library staff could offer to bring the reference books to the disabled person**

However, the service is not required to make changes which affect the fundamental nature of the business. For example, dim lighting could be considered essential to a nightclub even though it causes difficulties for someone with poor eyesight.

From 2004

Providers of goods, facilities, and services will have to make reasonable adjustments to their physical premises where this is needed to provide reasonable access to disabled people (for example, by installing ramps).

Selling or letting land or property:

It is unlawful for anyone who sells or lets land or property (and their agents) to discriminate unjustifiably against disabled people. For example, a landlord could not charge a disabled person a higher rent than he would charge anyone else.

A landlord who rents six or fewer rooms in his own home is not affected.

People selling or renting property do not currently have to make adjustments to the property to make it accessible.

How do we know what the DDA means?

The Government have published four documents which give further guidance on the meaning of the DDA: separate Codes of Practice in relation to employment, service delivery, schools and post 16 education, and, service delivery Guidance on the definition of disability. These documents can be used by tribunals or courts as guidance to interpret the law.

In addition case law has helped to clarify the meaning of the Act. The initial level of decisions – in tribunals or county courts – do not establish precedents. It is only when decisions are appealed to a higher level that an authoritative interpretation is set.

How are these rights enforced?

Disabled individuals who feel that they have been discriminated against can take legal proceedings against an employer or service provider.

Employment complaints must be taken to an employment tribunal. Complaints concerning services or the sale or rental of property must be taken to the county court. In most cases the complaint will be heard in the small claims section of the county court.

Legal Services Commission (Legal Aid) is not able to pay for representation in the employment tribunal or small claims section of the county court.

If an employment complaint succeeds the tribunal can award damages for any financial loss the disabled person has suffered and/or for injury to his/her feelings. There is no limit on the amount of damages that can be paid. The Government proposes to allow tribunals in the future to order re-instatement or re-engagement of an individual who has been dismissed because of discrimination.

Financial compensation can also be awarded for discrimination by service providers or landlords. The courts can also issue injunctions - court orders requiring a service provider to take, or to desist from taking, certain actions.

The Advisory, Conciliation and Arbitration Service (ACAS) provides conciliation in the employment field, helping employees and employers to reach a mutually satisfactory settlement without a hearing. There is a less comprehensive conciliation service for complaints regarding discriminatory services, run by the Disability Rights Commission.

Other measures in the act

Transport

New 'land based' public transport vehicles (trains, trams, buses, coaches and taxis) are covered by Part 5 of the

DDA in regulations. Two of the three sets have already been issued. The RVAR (Rail Vehicle Accessibility Regulations)1998 came into force in November 1998 and affect all new trains. The PSVAR (Public Service Vehicle Accessibility Regulations) 2000 affect new buses and coaches. Provision is also made in Part 5 for taxi regulations to be issued this has not yet happened - a second round of consultation is due later this year. Section 37 of the DDA which places a duty on licensed taxis to carry assistance dogs at no extra cost is already in force.

1.1

Education

The Special Educational Needs and Disability Rights in Education Act became law in May 2001. Certain sections extend the scope of the DDA, as it affects education:

- **the new act protects people who are defined as disabled by the DDA**
- **gives new responsibilities to all publicly funded FE and HE institutions, schools and local authorities not to discriminate against disabled students**
- **affects all education and training provided by these bodies, admissions to courses, exclusions, and the provision of other 'student services' e.g. residential accommodation, leisure facilities, catering and library facilities, etc.**
- **education providers may need to make adjustments to the above services which could include changes to policies and practices, changes to course requirements or work placements, changes to physical features of a building, the provision of interpreters or other support workers, the delivery of courses in alternative ways, or the provision of materials in alternative formats**

The Act ensures recognition of the needs of disabled people wishing to study and provision of better information for parents, pupils and students.

Developments

Disability rights taskforce

The Government's response to the Disability Rights Taskforce Report was to accept some of the proposals extending the DDA to include:

- **removing the justification for failure to make reasonable adjustments because this defence can be entirely covered by the need for adjustments only to be reasonable**
- **ensuring that all small employers and prospective employers are covered by Part II of the DDA**
- **ensuring that the following are protected from disability discrimination:**

- partners in partnerships of any size, as well as prospective partners;
- police officers (including the Ministry of Defence Police, British transport Police, Royal Parks Constabulary, and United Kingdom Atomic Energy Authority Constabulary);
- prison officers;
- fire-fighters (including Ministry of Defence Fire Service)
- barristers in chambers and barristers' pupils, and in Scotland, advocates' pupils;
- members of county, district and London borough councils;
- employees on board a ship, aeroplane or hovercraft registered in Great Britain (unless the employee does his/her work wholly outside Great Britain)

- **enabling employment Tribunals to order re-instatement or re-engagement in cases brought under the employment provisions of the DDA; this could increase the chances of disabled people returning to employment rather than being awarded compensation**

- **extending the protection of the DDA to people with cancer and HIV**

European dimension

The Employment Directive under Article 13 of the EC Treaty covers employment, occupational and vocational training. It requires Member States to introduce legislation protecting people from discrimination on the following grounds: disability, age, religion or belief, gender and sexual orientation. In relation to disability these must be implemented by 2006.This will require the UK to make minor changes to the DDA, but not significantly change it.

Help, advice and information can be obtained from the following organisations

- **Disability Rights Commission**
- **Employers' Forum on Disability**

(Contact details are provided at the back of this book).

A PRACTICAL GUIDE TO

adjustments in employment

The duty of reasonable adjustment

What is reasonable?

Preparing to make adjustments

1.2

Introduction

The Disability Discrimination Act (DDA) came into force on 2nd December 1996. It protects disabled people from discrimination in employment and requires employers to make 'reasonable adjustments' if disabled people are at a disadvantage in relation to other applicants or employees. Reasonable adjustments are a way of levelling the playing field for people with disabilities.

This section provides practical guidance on the kind of adjustments employers may have to make. It should help employers comply with the law but is principally designed to ensure that what they do reflects best practice and brings business benefit. It cannot precisely define 'reasonable' adjustment because that will depend on individual circumstances. Interpretation of the law will also depend on the rulings of employment tribunals and the courts, and it will take time for case law to develop.

The concept of adjustment is not new. For years employers have been making adjustments of various kinds which have enabled them to recruit, retain and develop disabled people – in the same way that they have made what are in effect 'adjustments' in other areas. They have, for example, allowed women returning from maternity leave to resume work on a part-time basis. Staff restaurants cater for ethnic, vegetarian and other dietary needs.

Many disabled people need no adjustments at all to enable them to work on equal terms with others. In many organisations the main adjustment necessary will be to move away from preconceived ideas about disabled people generally and to shift the focus to what the individual is capable of doing.

How employers are responding

Lewisham Council, which employs 10,500 people, has established processes for collecting, collating and co-ordinating information about adjustments. The aim is to spread good practice across the Council, ensure consistency in approach, monitor costs and solve at an early stage any problems that may arise.

1.2

The duty of reasonable adjustment

The duty of reasonable adjustment applies where any physical feature of the employer's premises, or any employment arrangements made by or on behalf of the employer, cause a substantial disadvantage to a disabled person compared to a non-disabled person. Employers will have discriminated if, in those circumstances, they fail to provide reasonable adjustment(s) and they cannot justify that failure.

'Reasonable adjustment' covers the whole range of employment, including:

- **recruitment and selection**
- **training**
- **promotion**
- **career development**
- **transfer**
- **retention – and what the DDA calls 'any other benefit'**

The duty of reasonable adjustment does not apply to the provision of benefits under an occupational pension scheme.

At present the employment provisions in the DDA only apply to employers of 15 or more people, regardless of the size of the individual workplace or branch. However, this threshold is to be removed by the end of 2004. All employers, irrespective of their size, are advised to follow the government's Code of Practice on eliminating discrimination against disabled people in employment.

Examples of adjustments

The DDA gives the following 12 examples of adjustments which employers may have to make.

A practical illustration is provided for each.

- **Making adjustments to premises**
  The direction in which a door opens is altered for a wheelchair-user

- **Allocating some of the disabled person's duties to another person**
  An applicant has a disability which causes vertigo. The job for which he is applying occasionally involves going onto an open roof, but he can otherwise do the job. The employer reallocates that minor requirement in the job to another employee

- **Transferring the disabled person to fill an existing vacancy**
  A sales representative develops multiple sclerosis and is unable to continue in the job because she has to give up driving. She is transferred to a vacant marketing post requiring computer skills, for which she is given training

- **Altering working hours**
  An employee with a mental health problem takes medication with side-effects which make it difficult for him to be alert in the morning. He is allowed to start later in the day and to work flexi-time

- **Assigning the disabled person to a different place of work**
  An employee develops a disability requiring use of a wheelchair. Her workstation on the third floor becomes inaccessible and so she is transferred to the ground floor

- **Allowing absence during working hours for rehabilitation, assessment or treatment**
  An employee who develops Parkinson's Disease requires a course of physiotherapy. He is given time off to attend for treatment

- **Giving or arranging training**
  A team of computer operators are given training on a new machine. To enable him to receive this training a visually impaired person is given additional software so that he can use a computer with speech output

- **Acquiring or modifying equipment**
  An employee with severe arthritis in the hands is given a portable computer to enable note-taking during training lectures

- **Modifying instructions or reference manuals**
  A new operating manual is introduced. A braille version is produced for a visually impaired employee. For an employee with a learning difficulty the supervisor provides oral instruction

- **Providing a reader or interpreter**
  A deaf employee who is being considered for promotion is to be interviewed by two senior managers. He lip-reads slowly which inhibits performance in an interview. To enable him to compete fairly with other candidates, a sign-language interpreter is provided for the day of the interviews

- **Providing supervision**
  A support worker is made available when needed to help an individual whose disability leads to uncertainty or lack of confidence

The DDA's list of 12 examples is not intended to be comprehensive. There will be situations where adjustments can be made which do not fall under any of the above headings.

How employers are responding

The Automobile Association (AA) has introduced a simple system of monitoring any adjustments that are made in the recruitment and appointment process. This also includes adjustments made to the jobs of people who become disabled. The personnel department, in collaboration with the line manager concerned, records details of how the adjustment came about and what the outcomes are. All requests for adjustments are documented. The aim is to share good practice and ensure consistency across the AA.

1.2

What is reasonable?

The DDA lists a number of factors likely to have a bearing on whether it is 'reasonable' for the employer to make an adjustment:

- **how effective the adjustment is in preventing the disadvantage**
- **how practicable it is**
- **its financial and other costs and how disruptive it is**
- **the employer's financial and other resources**
- **the availability of financial or other help**

When evaluating what is the reasonable cost of an adjustment, you should include the cost of recruiting (including staff time spent selecting and interviewing candidates), and training a replacement.

The Access to Work programme, run by the Employment Service, provides help towards the extra costs of employing someone with a disability. It is available to unemployed, employed and self-employed people and can apply to any job, full-time or part-time, permanent or temporary. The funding available depends on the employment status of the disabled individual at the time of the application. For those working for an employer for 6 weeks or more, it pays up to a maximum of 80% of the costs of many adjustments between £300 and £10,000 and 100% of those costing over £10,000.

For unemployed peole and people working for an employer for less than 6 weeks the programme pays 100% of approved costs.

The programme also pays 100% of approved costs, regardless of the employment status of the person, for support workers, fares to work and communicator support at interview.

Access to work support is for a maximum period of 3 years, after which it is reviewed. A person may still be eligible for assistance after this time. The availability of assistance from Access to Work could make 'reasonable' an adjustment that would otherwise be regarded as too costly for the employer. Further information about the Access to

Work Scheme can be obtained through the Disability Employment Adviser, at your local Jobcentre.

The cost of adjustments

The Department for Education and Employment Research Brief, No. 56 (March 1998), states "by far the most common cost band for adjustments introduced was from nil to £49".

How employers are responding

HSBC Bank plc have a central budget for funding adjustments that incur costs. This enables the bank to keep an eye on how and where adjustments are being introduced; helps to ensure consistency; and enables best practice to be shared throughout the organisation.

Preparing to make adjustments

You will need to consider whether adjustments are required when:

- **a disabled person applies for a job**
- **an existing employee develops a disability, or when the effects of a disability change or increase**
- **there is a change in what a disabled employee does, for example, when duties change, or when the individual is given a new job or a change of location**
- **when a disabled employee requires training**

You will also be required to consider making adjustments for temporary and contract workers.

The DDA says that an employer is not obliged to make an adjustment if there is no reason to suppose that an individual has a disability which is likely to affect his or her work. However, an employer must take all reasonable steps to find out whether this is the case. When recruiting, for example, you might invite applicants to indicate at the interview whether they require an adjustment to enable them to do the job. For existing employees your annual appraisal system could provide a similar opportunity.

The DDA does not require an employer to make changes in anticipation of employing a disabled person. An employer does not, for example, have to produce application forms in large print or braille until a visually impaired applicant asks for one. It is only sensible, however, to prepare for adjustments. For example, if you are introducing a new telecommunications system it could well be more cost effective in the long run to make it accessible to deaf people even if you have no deaf employees at the moment.

Job specifications can play a key role in identifying what adjustments, if any, are necessary to enable a disabled person to do a particular job. They should focus on the essential requirements of the post.

Routine selection tests should be reviewed to ensure that they are strictly relevant to the post(s) to be filled. The conditions in which the tests are taken may need to be adapted to take account of a disability. For example, a job applicant with a learning disability or a dyslexic applicant may need more time to do a test than is normally allowed.

Joint problem-solving

1.2

Because of their day-to-day experience, disabled people will usually be the experts on the effects of their impairment and how these can be overcome.

Discuss possible adjustments and engage in joint problem-solving. Be open to suggestions about how jobs or working arrangements might be done differently.

When adjustments have been identified, be specific and put decisions in writing, with a timetable if necessary. Recognise that needs may change, and set up a simple mechanism for reviewing adjustments periodically.

What if no adjustment is possible?

If no adjustment is possible which will enable a disabled person to perform the essential tasks of a job, there is no requirement to recruit that person. You will, however, need to be able to show that:

- **essential job requirements were identified**
- **possible adjustments were considered and discussed with the person**
- **expert advice, where possible, was sought**

Help, advice and information can be obtained from the following organisations

- **AbilityNet**
- **ACAS (The Advisory, Conciliation and Arbitration Service)**
- **Disability Rights Commission**
- **Employers' Forum on Disability**
- **Her Majesty's Stationary Office**
- **Jobcentre Plus: (formerly known as The Employment Service)**
- **Saville and Holdsworth**

(Contact details are provided at the back of this book).

A PRACTICAL GUIDE TO

management and the medical adviser

- When to seek medical advice
- Commissioning medical advice
- A disability management policy
- Disability-related assessment
- Briefing medical advisers
- Possible costs

1.3

This section aims to help employers use medical advice to best effect when managing disability in the workplace.

What the Act requires

Under the Disability Discrimination Act (1995) (DDA) it is unlawful for an employer to treat a disabled applicant or employee less favourably than others for a reason related to his or her disability, without justification.
An employer has a duty to make "reasonable adjustments" if a disabled applicant or employee is at a substantial disadvantage in relation to others. To justify less favourable treatment, an employer must show a "material and substantial" cause that cannot be resolved by reasonable adjustments. Anyone whose mental or physical impairment has a substantial adverse effect that lasts, or is expected to last, at least twelve months is protected under the Act. Who is or is not protected may not be obvious. Our advice is to take a positive attitude towards resolving problems rather than spending time and money trying to establish if someone is covered.

Medical advisers and disability

Decisions on employability are a managerial not a medical responsibility. A medical adviser's role is to assess risks, to make recommendations and to present the findings clearly. The employers must then decide on the acceptability of those recommendations in accordance with the DDA and other employment law. We refer to disability advisers as "medical advisers" in this briefing because it is the term most commonly used; however, advisers are not always medical doctors, but can be occupational health officers, disability employment advisers or other specialists referred to specifically elsewhere in this book.

When to seek medical advice

Often, what needs to be done in terms of adjustments is clear. Start by asking the individual, as a matter of course, "is there anything that would make it easier to do the job?" It is good practice to ask this, whether or not you think they have a disability. A disabled person may know exactly the adjustments they need, simply by exploring the working environment, and these might be very simple to arrange. When this is quite straightforward, there would be no need to call in a medical adviser.

You are more likely to want to call an expert if suitable adjustments are difficult to identify or hard to provide. When a person is newly disabled or has a fluctuating or progressive condition, and is not sure about what would enable them to do the job, you would naturally look for specialist expertise.

Whether you use a medical adviser or not, it is key to remember that you – as the employer – are responsible for making the necessary reasonable adjustments. What you do with advice is as important as the quality of that advice. We consider below when the advice provided is inappropriate.

1.3

Sandy v Hampshire Constabulary

Employers must not accept medical advice at face value

Mr Sandy had a back problem and partial hearing loss. While working for a year in a temporary post as a police station inquiry officer, he had five days absence, including four days for an ear operation. Mr Sandy applied for an equivalent post with a different force, Hampshire Constabulary, on a permanent basis. The force medical officer said Mr Sandy was unfit for this post, because his back injury would give rise to an unacceptable level of sickness. On this basis, Hampshire Constabulary withdrew a conditional offer of employment.

The medical officer had not examined Mr Sandy, nor obtained his attendance record. Sight of the record did lead to a revised opinion, but only after an alternative candidate had been appointed.

Mr Sandy challenged the treatment under the DDA. Hampshire Constabulary sought to defend its decision on the basis that the force had acted on medical advice, on good faith, and that the medical adviser's decision was justified because, although mistaken, it was based on genuine belief.

The tribunal found the decision arbitrary and speculative. While the personnel officer was right to take careful account of the medical officer's report, the employment tribunal said, it was also incumbent upon him to apply his own analysis and judgement. The personnel officer should have reflected that the applicant had successfully fulfilled his duties in the temporary post. Management was responsible for the decision, and had breached the DDA.

Commissioning medical advice

Ensure that your doctor understands:

- **that disability is a discrimination issue and that there is a duty to make reasonable adjustments**
- **the extent to which reasonable adjustments might enable a person to do a particular job (expertise on reasonable adjustments is critical in assessment)**
- **that referral for specialist medical advice may be necessary**

Historically, doctors tend to:

- **underestimate the skills and capacity of disabled people**
- **underestimate what can be achieved through adaptations at work**
- **overestimate the risks for the employer and the disabled person, regarded as a "patient"**
- **have views based on someone's medical history and make assumptions about an impairment generally, rather than assess the impact of a particular impairment on the particular person in the particular job, in the light of all the circumstances**

The extent to which someone is disabled often has as much to do with the environment, as with the individual's impairment. Therefore, it helps if medical advisers have some awareness of how to overcome environmental obstacles.

Reasonable adjustments

The need to consider reasonable adjustments is critical. Fast-changing technology can transform a person's capacity to work. Check that medical advisers have:

- **the expertise**
- **the time**
- **the relevant experience to advise on these themselves, or to provide sufficient information for a Disability Employment Adviser**

1.3

Forder v Southern Water

Medical Adviser fails to consider reasonable adjustments

Mr Forder had worked for Southern Water for over 20 years as a mechnical fitter. He had emphysema and was dismissed after refusing a job transfer that involved climbing ladders, he had said this would prove difficult for disability-related reasons.

The tribunal held that dismissal was not justified. The employer had neglected its duty to consider reasonable adjustments, including the possibility of re-assigning minor duties attached to the job. The occupational health officer had advised medical retirement, against Mr Forder's wishes, and admitted that reasonable adjustments had not been considered. The medical adviser argued that if Southern Water had wanted him to consider this issue, they should have told him so. Southern Water human resource manager had assumed that it was up to the medical adviser to state if reasonable adjustments were possible.

Since there had been no consultation with Mr Forder prior to his dismissal, either about changes to the job or alternative employment, the tribunal held the dismissal to have been unfair and discrimination to have occurred.

A disability management policy

The impact of a disability depends on the complex interplay between the person, the impairment, the environment and the particular requirements of the job.

Employers need to establish a policy framework for disability management. Policy and procedures on disability must correlate. It is important to review policies on recruitment, long-term absence, health and safety, medical retirement, capability and occupational health to ensure that they are compatible with the disability policy and reflect the requirements of the DDA. Sometimes it becomes necessary to revise health and fitness standards for particular jobs, where existing standards might wrongfully exclude a disabled person. The framework should designate responsibility for decisions, and specify the circumstances that trigger the commissioning of a medical report and its scope. (See Chapter 1.4 of this book – Health and Safety and the DDA)

Experiences of disability management in other countries, e.g., in Australia and Canada offer models of operation and evaluation. The National Institute of Disability Management and Research (NIDMR) in Canada suggests that success for disability management programmes can be judged by looking for:

- **an increased rate of successful return after long-term absence**

- a reduction of costs associated with disability in the workplace
- improvements in employee morale
- increased productivity

The crucial component is co-ordination of the many factors and personnel who may be involved. This is best accomplished by appointing a disability management co-ordinator.

The role of the disability management co-ordinator

The disability management co-ordinator is pivotal to the system, linking together opinions and expertise in assessment, operation and review (see "key players" below). The human resources manager often takes this role. A collaborative approach will be important, and there will be times when advisers need to cohere as a team, especially on policymaking, in review and in resolution of disagreement. It is the co-ordinator who guides the process as a "case manager".

The disability management co-ordinator might:

- **identify individuals who need disability management or support in return-to-work**
- **work closely with the person through assessment, planning, decision-making and review**
- **protect the individual's rights, assure confidentiality and explain these to the individual**
- **manage assessment, and commission specialist advice where needed**
- **brief advisers thoroughly**
- **co-ordinate the functional analysis of particular jobs, to include core competencies and capability standards required**
- **gather reports for cross-disciplinary review to interpret assessment adjustments, such as, equipment, changes to environment or modifications to the job - supported as appropriate by staff training**
- **document the process in relation to each individual to include any (material and substantial) justifications for less favourable treatment**
- **where a person cannot do a job, manage the process of retirement so that all understand the rationale**

Key players in disability management

The disability management team could involve any, or all of the following:

- **disabled individual**
- **disability management co-ordinator (possibly fulfilled by the human resources or occupational health manager)**

- **occupational health specialist**
- **human resources manager**
- **Disability Employment Adviser (DEA) based at the local Jobcentre - can offer a range of practical and financial assistance. The DEA may, in turn, refer to technical specialists to advise on equipment: aids may be supplied under the Access to Work scheme**
- **health and safety officer**

1.3

- **General Practitioner (GP)**
- **specialist medical adviser or para-medic such as occupational or physio-therapist or a psychiatric nurse**
- **ergonomics expertise – corporate approaches vary and may involve several departments; a specialist design consultant may be brought in**
- **line manager**
- **trade union representative**
- **other employee representatives**

A mix of people with this kind of range of responsibilities, perspectives and functions might more easily understand together the spread of health and safety, anti-discrimination and other employment regulations and how they apply.

Disability-Related Assessment

Any disability-related assessment will need to include advice on the availability of reasonable adjustments. Where less favourable treatment, such as dismissal or disciplinary proceedings or denial of promotion is contemplated, the assessment should include advice on the "material and substantial" reason under the terms of the DDA.

Factors that could affect someones employability include:

- **the skills, aptitudes and aspirations of the individual**
- **the precise nature of the impairment: how it limits function, and how the individual can manage**
- **the effectiveness of reasonable adjustments and the employer's expertise in making adjustments**
- **the nature of the environment in which a person needs to operate**
- **health and safety risks**

As disability concerns more than impairment, so assessment must include more than medical advice. Medical advisers should be encouraged to visit the site and observe the work in practice, where possible. Discussion with the individual and managers to explore fears and concerns is also helpful at a very early stage. When commissioning a GP as an adviser, offer to pay locum expenses to ensure the GP has the necessary time. It could make all the difference to the quality of the advice.

When planning the assessment:

- **identify the range of people who might contribute**
- **commission advisers and brief them thoroughly**
- **offer advisers access to the workplace and to managers who can further explain job requirements or demonstrate areas of concern**
- **review the assessment with the advisers and with the employee and make decisions**
- **put recommendations into practice with a strategy for review**
- **be aware that circumstances may change and a series of assessments over time may become necessary**

First stop: Jobcentre Plus

As we note at the start of this section, you would not always need a doctor as adviser. The first port of call in assembling advice for an assessment is often the Disability Employment Adviser (DEA) based at the local Jobcentre. DEAs help with technological aids, adaptations to the physical environment and modifications to the job or task distribution. They might also identify an appropriate expert on aids for particular impairments.

Choosing medical advisers

We recommend that employers use occupational health specialists wherever possible. They can be found through the Society of Occupational Medicine, which publishes regional lists of members, detailing their qualifications and work experience together with an explanation of what the qualifications mean. Qualifications to look for, usually held by full-time specialists, include: Associate Member, or Fellow of the Faculty of Occupational Medicine of the Royal College of Physicians (AFOM, MFOM and FFOM). A large company may have its own occupational health unit, or engage an occupational health specialist on a retainer basis.

There are by no means enough OH specialists to meet demand, but a growing number of GPs have the Diploma of Occupational Medicine (DOccMed).

Briefing medical advisers

When you refer someone to a medical adviser, you should supply objective and quantitative information about the job. A thorough job profile and briefing at this stage will help determine the quality of the final report.

The referral should:

- **describe the job precisely**
- **quote hours to be worked**

- **indicate physical requirements of the job, including stamina or strength required**

- **note intellectual and emotional demands, including stress factors**

- **indicate the employers expectations – what are the key outputs and what would qualify the employee for promotion?**

1.3

It might be helpful to issue medical advisers with a pro forma to make sure that the report covers the necessary ground. Questions could include:

- **what is this persons capability in relation to this job?**

- **what adjustments would enable this individual to do this job effectively?**

- **is there an underlying medical problem? Could medical intervention, change of medication, or specialist rehabilitation help the individual work to their full potential? (rehabilitation could itself be regarded as a reasonable adjustment)**

The role of the medical adviser

Advisers may be asked to perform any of a range of services, depending on the size of the organisation and its disability management infrastructure. A medical adviser might, for example:

- **produce a medical report on an individuals employability**

- **work with the co-ordinator in identifying appropriate adjustments**

- **assess adjustments in operation**

- **liaise with the employee (see section on confidentiality below)**

- **liaise with the employees own GP or consultant**

It helps if the medical adviser understands:

- **the requirements of the particular job**

- **the DDA**

- **the employers disability-related policies**

- **the range of technical aids and devices, and community or employment-related services available**

- **current thinking and best practice in disability management at work, with particular regard to early intervention, strategies on retention, planning return to work and reasonable adjustments**

Testing the medical advice

It is your duty as the commissioning employer to satisfy yourself about the quality of a doctors report. Consider, has the doctor:

- **examined the person?**

- **looked at the sickness record?**
- **recommended or sought further specialist advice if the disability was, for example, fluctuating, progressive or episodic in effect (such as epilepsy) or especially affected by the environment (visual or hearing impairment, asthma)?**
- **covered every aspect of your brief?**
- **understood the key requirements of the job?**
- **taken into account reasonable adjustments?**

Also, do you and the disabled individual understand what the medical adviser has said, and how he or she has justified the recommendations?

Beware of misplaced assumptions, either yours or the adviser's. No two people have the same experience of disability, and no two disabilities will have the same impact on an individual's capacity to work. Recommendations must be based on specifics relating to the individual and their capacity to do the job in question.

Holmes v Whittingham & Porter

When to go to a Specialist Consultant

Mr Holmes had worked as a labourer for Whittingham & Porter for 31 years. He experienced epilepsy involving occasional seizures with "robotic movement" but had never collapsed, until he did so on 6 March 1998. The employer suspended him from employment on the basis of a medical report from his GP, sent to the company medical adviser. Neither was a specialist in occupational medicine or epilepsy. Their concern was that Mr Holmes' job required him to go near hot metal and forging hammers. The GP said Mr Holmes would not be regarded fit for duties unless there were a further medical report stating that his epilepsy was controlled. Mr Holmes was dismissed.

The tribunal held that the medical adviser was inadequately qualified and found that Mr Holmes had been treated less favourably without adequate justification. The DDA claim succeeded.

1.3

Recruitment

Some employers may have developed medical assessment procedures, which required disabled people to attend inappropriate medical examinations. Blanket exclusions may have applied, which would now be unlawful. This is illustrated by the following case:

Eastabrook v Campbell Grocery Products

Mr Eastabrook is profoundly deaf in one ear and uses a hearing aid in the other. In response to an advertisement for temporary forklift truck drivers he disclosed his disability in an application form. Campbells Grocery Products interviewed Mr Eastabrook and sent him for a medical. He was told immediately that he would not pass the hearing test and therefore rejected for the job.

Mr Eastabrook went back to the Disability Employment Adviser at the JobCentre who contacted Campbells and asked them to reconsider in the light of the DDA. Campbells assured the DEA that they were well aware of the Act, and operating in accordance with it.

Six weeks later Mr Eastabrook sought work through an agency. The agency said Campbells was the only local option, approached them once more, and received the same response.

Mr Eastabrook brought a claim for disability discrimination. Initially Campbells sought to argue that he was not protected by the DDA. However, they subsequently admitted that his disability was covered, and that they had discriminated against him. They did not seek to justify refusing him employment. Mr Eastabrook was awarded £11,100 for loss of earnings and £2,500 for injury to feelings.

It is discriminatory to single out disabled job applicants by requiring more medical, or other information, than you would for a non-disabled applicant, unless the information relates directly to the position applied for. Employers may find that medical advice is not always the most appropriate or helpful. If, say, a blind person applied for a management post, it would not be appropriate to obtain a medical report detailing the visual impairment. Instead, you should contact the Disability Services Team (through the local Jobcentre) for an assessment of practical adjustments to assist the applicant in the job. Equipment is available under the Access to Work scheme. (For more information see chapter 1.6 – Managing Recruitment and the fact sheet on Access to Work.)

Managing Absenteeism

Managing long-term absenteeism will inevitably take employers into DDA territory: best and most prudent practice is to develop policies and procedures so that long-term absence is always managed as though the duty to make adjustments applied (see Chapter 1.5 – Managing Sickness Absence). A similar team approach works well in arriving at appropriate adjustments, as in the following case:

Query

An employee with asthma is a good worker, but a pattern of absenteeism has emerged. Every year between September and April he is absent for about 30 days (not consecutive). What

reasonable adjustments might the employer introduce?

Response

Climate changes may affect severity and frequency of the asthma attacks, resulting in more sickness absence. Speak to the employee and establish where the main problem lies in his or her doctor's opinion. Do they think the asthma is worsened by external factors or by the working environment? If a hazard within the workplace acts as a trigger it's maybe possible to move it to another part of the building. Could better medication or medical rehabilitation be useful?

Possible adjustments to consider might include: relocation, working from home when necessary, increasing the ventilation around the workstation, allowing more than the usual sick leave, or unpaid leave for sickness over and above an agreed period. The employee might have further suggestions. These measures would have to be viewed in the light of the employee's continued capability to meet his particular job requirements.

Medical Retirement

Too often in the past there were assumptions that the onset of disability inevitably led to medical retirement. Where retirement is not what the disabled employee wants, these assumptions could be successfully challenged under the DDA. Employers must thoroughly investigate options for reasonable adjustments and opportunities for redeployment before considering retirement.

Brown v South Bank University

Wrongful Grounds for Involuntary Medical Retirement

Ms Brown has multiple sclerosis. In 1994 she was given permission to work at home for two days in any week. She was off work for three months at the beginning of 1997. On her return, South Bank University held a number of meetings with her to discuss her problems and sought medical reports. Ms Brown's GP reported her fit for work and recommended that she work three days per week in the office and two days per week at home, a view supported by a consultant neurologist. The University told Ms Brown that it was a condition of her continued employment that she work in the University office five days a week and briefed their own medical adviser on this basis. Since Ms Brown was unable to attend full time, the medical officer recommended medical retirement, which Ms Brown accepted.

Ms Brown's disability discrimination claim was successful. The employment tribunal found that Ms Brown did not leave work voluntarily. She had to choose between dismissal or early retirement. The University had given Ms Brown less favourable

1.3

treatment and failed to justify this, for the tribunal did not accept the employers' claim that attendance in the office five days a week was necessary.

Confidentiality

The issue of confidentiality is important and complex. Any medical adviser will be working within legal and ethical constraints, they must guarantee confidentiality to employees and also inform employers of the need for reasonable adjustments.

1.3

The DDA requires employers to consider reasonable adjustments wherever they know, or could reasonably be expected to have known, that an employee or applicant is at a substantial disadvantage as a result of a disability.

When a medical adviser is commissioned by an employer, the employer will be deemed to know about any disability which an employee or applicant discloses to that adviser: the employer's obligation under the DDA to consider adjustments comes into force, even if the disabled person insists on confidentiality.

Part of the medical adviser's duty of care to an employee or job applicant is to advise them of the advantages and disadvantages of disclosing a disability. If the disabled person insists on confidentiality, but the physician considers disclosure to be necessary, compromise might be sought. If the individual does not agree with the compromise, the physician should document the effort to argue this course. Employment tribunals would be expected to take this into account.

The compromise may well have been that the diagnosis or "label" of a disability is not disclosed, and the employer advised only of the adjustment needed.

Possible costs

The British Medical Association (BMA) issues to medical professionals a schedule of "private and professional" suggested fees for work undertaken by doctors outside the NHS. These are intended as guidelines only: Doctors may charge more or less, and costs will vary according to what is involved. Fees for site visits and further consultation would be "by negotiation". The sums quoted below are BMA guidelines and apply to employers other than local authorities or central government. The BMA suggests that GPs use their own private rate for work. The sums are correct at the time of going to press (2002).

GPs hourly rate for work in the surgery: £144 per hour

Medical examination and report: £108 per hour

Extract from medical records only: £36.50

Below are the rates for Occupational Physicians (consultants) as NHS employees.

Session of one hour: £28.80 – £38.10
Session of 3.5 hours: £101 – £133

Help, advice and information can be obtained from the following organisations

- **Employers' Forum on Disability**
- **Jobcentre Plus**

(Contact details are provided at the back of this book).

References:

- **National Institute of Disability Management and Research: Disability Management in the Workplace**
- **Institute of Personnel Development: Guide on Occupational Health and Organisational Effectiveness**
- **Faculty of Occupational Medicine: The Disability Discrimination Act 1995, A Guide for Occupational Physicians**
- **The Society of Occupational Medicine:The DDA**
- **Croner's: How should employers handle medical advice in relation to the DDA ? (Susan Scott-Parker (1998)**

A PRACTICAL GUIDE TO

health and safety and the DDA

Health and Safety and the DDA

Risk Assessment

Reasonable and Reasonably Practicable Adjustments

Residual Health and Safety Risks

Questions and Answers

1.4

The Employers' Forum on Disability gratefully acknowledges the substantial help it has received from Dr. William Davies FFOM LLM, specialist in Occupational Medicine, in preparing this guidance.

The DDA

The Disability Discrimination Act 1995 aims to eliminate discrimination against disabled people. Part II of the Act introduces a general principle of non-discrimination into employment and imposes a duty on employers to make reasonable adjustments to working arrangements. Unlike other anti-discrimination legislation, the DDA allows for circumstances under which discrimination can be justified for reasons that are "material to the circumstances of the particular case and substantial". One possible area of justification for not employing disabled employees or job applicants lies in health and safety, if it can be shown that there is an unacceptable risk in the workplace to the disabled employee's own or others' safety.

In the vast majority of cases health and safety presents no barriers to the employment of disabled individuals. This section offers guidance on the interaction between the DDA and other legal duties of the employer to ensure the health and safety of all employees in the minority of cases where health and safety concerns arise. It suggests ways in which potentially conflicting duties of the employer may be reconciled in practice.

Health and Safety

By law, employers have a duty to provide a safe system of work for all employees. The Health & Safety at Work Act 1974 (HASWA), imposes several

1.4

statutory duties upon the employer; for example, the employer must "ensure, so far as is reasonably practicable, the health, safety and welfare at work of all employees". The Management Regulations give guidance to employers on meeting this duty to provide safe working practices. They require an employer to make a suitable and sufficient assessment of the risks to the health and safety of their employees. The Approved Code of Practice to the regulations states that employers, in undertaking their risk assessment, should identify groups of workers who might be particularly at risk. It refers to disabled staff as one of these groups.

Breach of this duty may lead to an improvement or prohibition notice being imposed on an employer or a criminal prosecution. Breach of more specific duties may also give rise to civil action against an employer.

Fulfilling your responsibilities under Health and Safety and the DDA

Situations may arise whereby employers believe they cannot meet their statutory duties under health and safety law if they employ a disabled person in a particular job.

However, if an employer refuses to employ or retain a disabled person and the reasons are ill founded, this may lead to the employer being taken to tribunal under the DDA.

Where health and safety is put forward as the reason for refusal to employ an individual, be sure that the reason is justifiable.

Section 6 of the DDA requires employers to make "reasonable adjustments" to working arrangements or physical features of premises which place disabled persons at a substantial disadvantage compared to non-disabled persons. Therefore, before refusing employment to a disabled person on H & S grounds, an employer must investigate whether a reasonable adjustment can resolve the problem.

To meet their obligations under both Health & Safety and the DDA employers would be advised to:

- **make an individual, objective and competent assessment of any risk that may be associated with employment of the particular disabled person**
- **implement or consider "reasonable adjustments" which would reduce or remove the risk**
- **do all that is "reasonably practicable" to remove the risk in the case of disabled persons already in employment**
- **deal reasonably with any cases involving residual risks**

Individual and competent risk assessment

Depending on the circumstances, this may range from a straightforward discussion with the disabled person on the effects of his or her disability, to a specialist medical assessment or the involvement of other health or assessment professionals.

Employers will need to evaluate the circumstances, decide on the type of assessment required and the need for specialist help from for example, occupational health practitioners, health & safety consultants and ergonomists.

when conducting a risk assessment, those involved must:

- **focus on facts, not assumptions**
- **assess the individual and avoid blanket restrictions**
- **discuss with the individual how limitations may be overcome**
- **apply best medical evidence on prognosis and associated occupational hazards/risks**
- **duly consult with other practitioners**
- **relate the individual to the essential requirements of the job**
- **consider all relevant occupational factors**
- **identify the actual duration and frequency of hazardous situations**
- **identify potential adjustments**

Reducing risk through reasonable adjustments

Good employment practice which enables the safe employment of disabled persons frequently depends on actions and arrangements which are called "reasonable adjustments" under the DDA. The Act places an obligation on employers to make such adjustments whenever it is reasonable to do so. Guidance on what is reasonable is provided within the Act itself and in the accompanying Code of Practice.

Reducing risk through reasonable practicable adjustments

Health and Safety law is intended to protect people's health and safety from risks arising from work activities. A person's disability may put him/her at greater risk from a particular work activity than their non-disabled colleagues. The employers' wide-ranging duty under HASWA to ensure so far as is reasonably practicable the health safety and welfare of all employees will include the requirement to adjust the workplace to reduce risks so far as is reasonably practicable. In practice therefore the Act requires reasonably practicable adjustments to be made, although this is not a term used in the statute. This requirement is an enabling and accommodating provision which , applying to all employees, both complements and supplements the DDA. The reasonable practicability of adjustments is determined on the basis of risk/cost-benefit analysis.

1.4

In many cases reasonably practicable adjustments will be the same as reasonable adjustments. In some circumstances, however, it is possible that tribunals and courts may apply different criteria. The "Guidance on Health & Safety at Work Act 1974" indicates that the financial standing of the employer is not relevant to the judgement of reasonable practicability. On the other hand, the DDA Code of Practice states "it is more likely to be reasonable for an employer with substantial financial reserves to make an adjustment with a significant cost than for an employer with few resources". Arguably therefore, the duty to make adjustments under Health & Safety law may be more stringent than under the DDA.

The law has yet to address this comparison but in any event where health and safety is an issue, both the duties under the DDA and under health and safety law are relevant. The employers should be clear that they must fully explore the potential of both of these duties to eliminate the risks in order to avoid unfair treatment.

It is also worth noting that whilst employers have a duty to make reasonable adjustments only in respect of individuals who fall within the definition of disability given in the DDA, any employee with any disability which has Health & Safety implications is protected by the duty to make reasonably practicable adjustments.

Adjustments in action

Arrangements for a person with a history of schizophrenia and irrational behaviour, but now on a successful treatment regime, might include reviews at suitable intervals by an occupational health practitioner; good liaison with the general practitioner and specialist, education and co-operation of working colleagues and regular management feedback. Such measures could ensure employment in many occupations in the manufacturing and service sectors which might otherwise be deemed unsuitable on health and safety grounds.

Modifying a job description to remove non-essential, but potentially hazardous duties may allow employment with minimal disruption, e.g. removal of the occasional requirement to lift in a person with arthritis, or the removal of work at heights for the employment of a person with epilepsy.

Replacing a sensitising or irritant product with an alternative, may, together with health surveillance, enable an employee with asthma or eczema to continue working as a paint sprayer or cleaner.

An employee of a small car components factory has a substantial hearing impairment but is unable to wear hearing protection because it impairs communication. There is concern that noise exposure from nearby machinery may cause further damage.

The Health & Safety advisor and occupational physician recommend that compliance with Health & Safety law could be achieved by the installation of sound barriers and regular audiometric surveillance.

Because of the considerable expense involved, the Managing Director takes further advice and concludes that the recommended measures may not be required as reasonable adjustments on cost grounds, but to avoid a breach of Health & Safety law it would be prudent to implement them as reasonably practicable adjustments.

Dealing with residual health and safety risks

Despite adjustments, the employment of a disabled person may still present Health & Safety risks to the individual or to others. Unacceptable residual risks, properly assessed as such under health & safety law, will be justification for dismissal under the DDA.

However, it is important to remember that risks may embrace a spectrum from trivial to serious. The question will therefore arise for employers, "what is acceptable or unacceptable?" This is a complex area and there is little guidance. Nevertheless the DDA will require employers to justify decisions and important principles of good practice in the following areas should be considered.

Management and medical responsibilities

Human resource managers often ask a doctor to assess fitness for work where the employment of a person with a medical condition may give rise to risks. This does not mean that the decision on employability is a medical responsibility. The doctor's role is to assess the risks and present them as clearly as possible. The employer must then decide on acceptability of risks in compliance with the DDA, health and safety law and employment law. Specialist occupational physicians, however, may be able to assist employers in deciding on what level of risk is acceptable.

Hazard and risk in perspective

An awareness of key Health and Safety concepts is essential if HR managers are to understand what is being assessed under Health and Safety law:

- **hazard – the potential for harm**
- **risk – the probability of harm occurring from a hazard**

- **negligible risk – the most widely held view in the context of health & safety is an annual risk of less than 1 in a million**

The hazard may be ranked according to the severity of the potential harm. The risk may be ranked according to the probability that harm will occur.

Risk/cost-benefit balance

1.4

Health and Safety law recognises that it not always possible nor reasonably practicable to eliminate risk. The concept of using a risk/cost-benefit balance to judge what is or is not reasonably practicable has been long established by case law (Edwards v National Coal Board 1949) in a way which can help employers distinguish between acceptable and unacceptable residual risks.

The employer has to make a computation in which the amount of risk is placed on one side of the scale and is balanced against the sacrifice in money, time or trouble involved in avoiding that risk. Factors which will weigh in favour of employment include the cost to the employer of losing a valuable employee or potential employee. If it is shown that there is a gross disproportion in the balance, and the risk is insignificant in proportion to the cost, then the employer has shown that dismissing the employee to eliminate the residual risk would not be necessary to achieve compliance with the duty to reduce risk so far as a is reasonably practicable.

With the Disability Discrimination Act important additional factors to consider are the human and financial costs in denying the disabled person employment. Existing policy and precedents regarding acceptability of risks in society may be helpful but the Employment Appeal tribunal has held that the DDA imposes a duty on employers and tribunals to balance the interests of employer and employee. In Baynton v Saurus the employer failed to justify selecting a disabled employee for redundancy because it had not given weight to his interests in remaining in work.

In the UK this type of risk/cost-benefit appraisal is relatively undeveloped, but the Disability Discrimination Act now provides employers with a powerful incentive to exploit its potential in the interests of both disabled people and organisations.

Risk to others

The law understandably sets a high standard for preventing risks to others, but this will not justify over-zealous discrimination for trivial hazards or the remote possibility of injury. For example, in teaching, the health care professions, manufacturing and many other occupations, perceived hazards of epilepsy are often found to be trivial when properly assessed and employment should not be prohibited.

It has been suggested that even serious hazards may be disregarded when, on the basis of a competent assessment, the risks are found to be negligible and all reasonably practicable precautions have been applied. Guidance on assessing the fitness of fire fighters with diabetes for example has acknowledged this principle.

The extent to which minor or moderate risks to others of low probability would be acceptable will depend on the outcome of a risk/cost benefit computation.

DDA Case Summary

Mr. Roberts was dismissed after 11 days working for ASD plc as a crane driver. The reason given in his letter of dismissal was that his hearing impairment created greater Health & Safety problems than had been appreciated when he was appointed. The issue for the tribunal was whether this treatment was justified under the DDA i.e. did the employer have a material and substantial reason for the dismissal?

Mr. Roberts had successfully worked for 8 years in a similar job with another employer, before losing his job when the factory closed. During this time he had gained an NVQ, which included "working safely in an industrial environment". During initial training Mr Robert's supervisor told him that he was doing very well, better than his hearing colleague who had been taken on at the same time. In particular he had computer skills which enabled him to help the other new employee. He was also able to hear machinery, and the approach of a forklift truck. Nevertheless, following one incident in which Mr Roberts had difficulty understanding instructions, his supervisor recommended his employment be terminated because he could not work adequately as part of a team.

It was at this point that the Health & Safety manager was consulted. He was concerned that the applicant would not be able to hear a shouted warning in an emergency. The steel sections he was shifting would cause serious injury or death if they fell on a person. He was also concerned that Mr Roberts would not be able to hear the horn of a truck, and would be in danger if one emerged from a concealed opening.

Mr Roberts claimed that his dismissal constituted disability discrimination. The tribunal did not accept that employer's reasons were material or substantial. They pointed to Mr Robert's previous experience of working in an industrial environment as sufficient to equip him with the means to avoid the hazard present in this job. "Whilst we acknowledge that there were and would continue to be difficulties of communication on occasions, we find that the need for much oral communication has been exaggerated by the respondent. Skilled workers operating in pairs learn to operate as a team without the need for much oral communication."

They felt that any impact which communication difficulties had on efficiency would not be significant.

They accepted that the consequences of any safety lapse would be very serious but asked whether the risk was "substantial or theoretical". They felt that given Mr Roberts awareness of his own disability, and the need to use eyesight to compensate, that the risk was theoretical. Mr Roberts therefore won his claim for disability discrimination.

1.4

Autonomy and risk to self

How should an employer respond where a residual risk has been properly identified, but is confined to the disabled employee themselves?

Here the risk/cost-benefit balance should reflect the wishes of the disabled employee. A full discussion with the individual should explain the nature and extent of the risk. An occupational health physician may be well placed to discuss relevant issues with the employee. Where the employee decides that the benefits of working outweigh the risks, his/her self-determination should be respected wherever possible. The relationship between the common law duty of care and an individual's freedom of choice is complex and you may want to seek legal advice. However, The Health and Safety at Work Act 1974 introduces general duties on all employees at work:

- **to take reasonable care for the health and safety of himself and of other persons who may be affected by his acts or omissions at work; and**
- **as regards any duty or requirement imposed on his employer or any other person by or under any of the relevant statutory provisions, to co-operate with him so far as is necessary to enable that duty or requirement to be performed or met**

The employer must do all that is reasonably practicable to eliminate risk, but this does not imply an absolute duty to remove risk. Case law has established that it is lawful for employers and their employees to accept even serious residual health and safety risks inherent in dangerous occupations providing the condition of reasonable practicability has been complied with.

The same principle may apply to additional risk because of the increased susceptibility of the particular employee. The special risk of injury to an employee with a known disability is a relevant consideration in determining the precautions which the employer should make to meet his duty of care. It does not, however, preclude employment. Where employers have acted reasonably to reduce risk and the employee is informed about this residual risk, an action in negligence for resulting harm will fail. Cases have established that there is no duty at common law to dismiss an employee rather than retain him because there might be some risk.

The DDA and Justification

Jones v The Post Office

Mr Jones was diagnosed as having insulin dependant diabetes in 1997. The Post Office's policy at that time was that anyone who received insulin treatment was not fit to continue with any driving duties for the business. Mr Jones brought a complaint of disability discrimination and the Post Office reconsidered its policy. It determined, after taking medical advice, that Mr Jones would be able to return to limited driving duties provided that these did not exceed two hours in any 24-hour period. In addition, the Post Office specified that he should be allowed

(i) time to take appropriate steps to control his diabetes, such as monitoring his blood sugar and taking additional meal breaks as necessary

(ii) flexibility to limit his driving should he feel unwell; and that in addition

(iii) he should present himself for a review of his medical condition at least every 6 months

Mr Jones accepted the above conditions but maintained that the continued restriction on his driving was still discriminatory. The Post Office accepted that the restriction was less favourable treatment but argued that they were justified because they were acting on medical advice. Mr Jones had medical advice that contradicted this and so argued that the Post Office was not justified. He was successful before the Employment Tribunal who preferred his medical expert's evidence which was based on the latest research but which had not been put to the Post Office before the Tribunal hearing.

Risk Assessments

The case was then appealed to the EAT and eventually to the Court of Appeal both of which overturned the Employment Tribunal decision. The Court of Appeal held that where an employer has undertaken a properly conducted risk assessment which:

- **provides a reason which is both material and substantial (the words in the DDA) and**

- **is not irrational**

then the employer is entitled to rely on that reason (the risk assessment) to justify less favourable treatment.

The Court of Appeal did go onto say that if the employee disagrees with the employer's medical advice and produces evidence of his own which is shown to the employer, this must be considered i.e. the employer should do another risk assessment.

1.4

Accepting Risk

The principles outlined above should usually determine if the risk is acceptable. If not, the employer will have to make a judgement; the overriding principle should be to act reasonably taking into account all relevant considerations and responsibilities. Whether the conclusion is then to employ or not to employ, the outcome would be equitable and legally sustainable and would represent best practice in a challenging area of human resource management.

Example

Steven, a recently qualified civil engineer who has epilepsy applied for a post as a project worker. Because of the hazards presented whilst working near moving plant machinery or at heights, the recruitment standards for the post adopted by the company excluded employment of applicants with epilepsy. The Health & Safety Adviser confirmed that, over a period of months, work was likely to involve many hours when these hazards would exist and rejection was necessary under Health & Safety Law. However, to ensure compliance with the DDA, the Personnel Officer requested:

1 a management report on the practicalities and cost of eliminating the hazards from the post

2 a specialist medical assessment of his prognosis and its relevance to the responsibilities of the post.

The management report concluded that whilst the work in hazardous situations could not be eliminated, it could be substantially reduced with comparatively little cost by reallocating responsibilities involving working at heights to other members of the team and rescheduling duties in the vicinity of plant machinery to times when the machines would not be operating. Hazardous work could effectively be minimised to no more than a few hours annually.

The specialist medical report identified that his epilepsy was well controlled and placed the annual risk of seizure recurrence between 1 in 3 and 1 in 5.

The reports enabled the personnel officer, the management team and the individual to agree that with reasonable adjustments and a review if circumstances changed, the residual risks to the applicant of accident or injury would be well below that accepted on a daily basis in activities such as driving, and the risks to others would be negligible. Employment was considered not to be in conflict with the Health & Safety at Work Act and discrimination under the DDA was not justified.

Questions and Answers

Q. How should human resource managers challenge medical advisers who do not seem to work to the same understanding of the DDA/best practice?

A. Establish that the medical adviser has:

- the relevant qualifications and experience and is familiar with the DDA
- a clear understanding of the distinction between medical and management responsibilities
- made an individual and competent risk assessment
- given due consideration to adjustments options
- not made assumptions about the acceptability/ unacceptability of any residual risks

Q. Do fire regulations preclude wheelchair users from using, say, the 6th floor?

A. There are no regulations automatically preclude a disabled person from using any part of a building. Building Regulations impose a requirement on access facilities for disabled people.

British Standard 5588, imposes requirements on escape provisions for disabled people. These are:

- the provision of a suitable lift, installed to the standards laid down in British Standard 5588 part 8, or
- the provision of "refuges" (safe areas) within protected stairway enclosures and a management led evacuation plan
- details of requirements should be confirmed with your Building Control Officer and your local Fire Safety Officer

Q. Are obligations to customers different than to employees?

A. Although detail of legal obligations is framed slightly differently to customers than employees, in practice they are likely to be broadly comparable

Q. Our Health and Safety manager says that we cannot assist a disabled colleague out of his car, or up the stairs in case we injure ourselves

A. Your health and safety adviser may be making a misguided and unjustified assumption. The provision of assistance for a disabled colleague in this situation may be seen as a reasonable adjustment. To comply with health and safety responsibilities, a risk assessment in accordance with the Management of Health and Safety at Work Regulations and the Manual Handling Regulations should identify what is necessary to avoid injury to yourselves or to your disabled colleague. Measures might include training in lifting techniques, provision of mechanical aids or non-involvement of any colleagues at special risks. Normally such measures would be regarded as reasonable adjustments or as reasonably practicable safeguards so, unless there are exceptional circumstances, the approach suggested by your health and safety adviser would probably be unlawful.

1.4 Help, advice and information can be obtained from the following organisations

- **Centre for Accessible Environments**
- **Disability Rights Commission**
- **Employers' Forum on Disability**
- **RADAR**

(Contact details are provided at the back of this book).

References

1 Davies J and Davies W, "Reconciling risk and the employment of disabled persons in a reformend welfare state". Industrial Law Journal, vol 29 (4), Dec 2000, pp347-377.

2 The Management of Health and Safety at Work Regulations 1992 SI 1992/2051

3 5 Steps to Risk Assessment. HSE Books, PO Box 1999, Sudbury, Suffolk CO10 6FS. Tel: 01787 881165

4 "Assessing Fitness for Work", William Davies, ABC of Work Related Disorders, British Medical Journal, Vol.313, 12 October 1996, pages 934-938.

5 "Endocrine Disorders", chapter 12, Medical Aspects of Fitness for Firefighting. Guidance issued by the Association of Local Authority Medical Advisors 1997

6 British Standard 5588: Fire precautions in the design and construction of buildings, Part 8, code of practice for means of escape for disabled people.

7 The Manual Handling Operations Regulations 1992 SI 1992/2793

A PRACTICAL GUIDE TO

managing sickness absence

- Practical procedures
- Assessments
- Sickness policies
- Reasonable adjustments
- Termination of contract

1.5

This section provides practical guidance for employers on specific topics relating to the employment of disabled people. It will be useful for personnel, human resources, occupational health, recruitment and training specialists as well as for line managers.

The guidance identifying three distinct types of sickness absence in this section can be used as a best practice approach. Your company may, however, already have in place good procedures and designated people to contact at key stages. In any case, this guidance can be used to review the company's approach to sickness absence, and the rest of the paper used to back up existing policy.

Introduction

There are three main types of sickness absence which require specific managerial procedures, and differ from non health and non disability related absences. These are:

1. **Long term sickness absence – known length [see page 51]**
2. **Long term sickness absence – unknown length [see page 52]**
3. **Periodic sickness absences [see page 53]**

Disability Discrimination Act

Under the Disability Discrimination Act it is unlawful for an employer to treat a disabled applicant for a job, or an employee, less favourably for a reason related to his/her disability without justification. An employer also has a duty to make reasonable adjustments to prevent an employee from being placed at a substantial disadvantage by any physical feature of the premises or by working arrangements.

1.5

When deciding whether or not an adjustment is reasonable an employer should consider:

- **the effectiveness of the adjustment in preventing the disadvantage**
- **the practicality of the adjustment**
- **the financial and other costs of the adjustment and the extent of any disruption caused**
- **the extent of the employer's financial or other resources**
- **the availability to the employer of financial or other assistance to help make an adjustment, for example through the Access to Work scheme and the support of the Employment Services' Disability Service Teams**

The DDA defines a disabled person as someone with a physical or mental impairment, which has a substantial and long-term adverse effect on their ability to carry out normal day-to-day activities. Someone on long-term sick leave or who has periodic sickness absences may not, at first, appear to meet this definition of disability. However, because the definition is so broad and because it is difficult to predict whether the absences may become disability related in the future, our guidance on sickness absence is for the employer to err on the side of best practice. It is always better to treat an employee who is off sick for a long period of time or has periodic sickness absences as though they are disabled and may therefore need reasonable adjustments. Note that in the case of Heinz v Kendrick, the EAT decided that the employer had sufficient knowledge of the manifestations of Mr Kendrick's condition to have discriminated against him by dismissing him for being off sick, even though the disability itself was not diagnosed until after his dismissal.

The employer should discuss with the employee whether any reasonable adjustments would:

- **enable the employee to return to work; or**
- **reduce the number or length of periodic absences; or**
- **help the employer to accommodate the periodic absences**

Remember that reasonable adjustments may prevent sickness absence in the first place, as well as enabling employees to carry out their jobs more effectively, for example adapted keyboards and voice-recognition software may help to prevent, or limit Repetitive Strain Injury (RSI).

Inter–departmental co-ordination

Employers will no doubt be committed to practices that seek to retain employees and profit from the proven cost benefits of retention. Effective management of sickness absence results from regular discussions with the person and an inter-departmental approach – bringing together experts from, for example, Human Resources and Occupational Health departments to discuss with the individual what policies can be put in place and what procedures will be followed.

Practical procedures

Managers should have training to deal with sickness absence in a clear and consistent manner, yet still be flexible enough to judge each case on an individual basis. Employees must be informed about both organisational procedures and their own responsibilities, for example that they should notify their line manager as soon as possible on the first day of sickness.

The employer should actively manage sickness absence by maintaining a positive dialogue with the employee when he or she is absent from work for a long period. The employer needs to understand the impact of the symptoms (and their treatment) that are keeping the employee away from work. This will help inform discussions about reasonable adjustments that might enable the employee to return to work as soon as possible.

The line manager in conjunction with human resources, Disability Employment Advisers and Occupational Health specialists may need to review duties that the employee has previously performed, once they have returned to work. This provides an opportunity for the duties to be adapted for the current employee as a reasonable adjustment. It will also benefit future employees if the current work arrangements have created an unhealthy workplace and could potentially lead to future sickness absence.

There should be a nominated person in a senior position who is kept fully informed about the employee's situation and any reasonable adjustments that are being made.

Health assessment

A health assessment or a report from the employee's own doctor may help to determine how long the employee will be off work and give a more detailed analysis of the employee's impairment. The employee should be asked to give consent for the employer to obtain a report from the employee's GP or specialist. The employer can also ask the employee to undergo an independent health assessment with a medical adviser of the employer's choosing; however, care should be taken to ensure that the adviser is an appropriate specialist.

The health adviser may suggest that the employee should retire early on ill-health grounds. Before acting on this advice the employer should ensure that the medical adviser has a good working knowledge of the DDA and is well briefed on what the employee's job entails. The adviser needs to be able to ask the right questions, refer to the job description and know about issues such as reasonable adjustments and redeployment. Retiring an employee on health grounds is not a cheap option; the Post Office carried out a survey that found that it costs them up to £80,000 to medically retire an employee.

For more information on how to brief a medical adviser, see Chapter 1.3 of this book: A practical guide to management and the medical adviser.

Brown v South Bank University

This case illustrates the need for the employer's own medical adviser to be briefed in light of the DDA so that an employee is not retired on medical grounds when a reasonable adjustment would have enabled the employee to return to work.

Ms Brown, who has multiple sclerosis, had been off sick for three months. When she was due to return to work she was seen by the employer's medical adviser who had been told that Ms Brown's position required her to work five days a week. Ms Brown could not work for this length of time and so the medical adviser recommended that she retire early on ill-health grounds. The tribunal ruled that Ms Brown had not left work voluntarily; she only had a choice between dismissal or early retirement. She had been unjustifiably treated less favourably because of her disability. The Tribunal did not accept the employers' claim that attendance at work five days a week was necessary.

1.5

Risk assessment

An employer may have health and safety concerns, particularly if an employee returns to work with a recently acquired disability. Reasonable adjustments should be considered first, with a discussion with the employee. If this does not allay health and safety concerns, advice could be gained from a specialist medical assessment or the involvement of other health professionals.

Employers will need to evaluate the circumstances, decide on the type of assessment required and the need for specialist help from, for example, occupational health practitioners, health and safety consultants and ergonomists. If health and safety is put forward as the reason for refusing to retain an employee, the reason has to be justifiable, otherwise the employer may be in breach of the DDA.

For more information on health and safety, see Chapter 1.4 of this book: A practical guide to Health and Safety & the DDA.

Sickness policies and record keeping

Policies which predate the introduction of the DDA, or which do not specifically address the legislation, may now result in the employer being in breach of the DDA.

Recording sickness absence

An employee's sickness records should differentiate between disability related and non-disability related absences. The way absences are recorded should be regularly monitored to ensure they are accurate. The employee may be reluctant to disclose the real reason for a period of absence where this is disability related. Asking why the employee was off sick on each occasion however, gives the employee an opportunity to disclose a disability and discuss any adjustments, if for example the sickness absences are being caused by a working arrangement. Remember that employees may not use the word "disabled" or even consider themselves to be disabled. The person may nevertheless need adjustments and may also meet the definition of disability contained in the DDA.

Any action taken with regard to an employee's absences should be recorded. A copy of the records should be kept in a central location, for example the Human Resources department. If an employee moves positions within an organisation it is important that recorded sickness absence and any adjustments that have been made can be picked up by the new management and are not lost as the person changes role.

Using information on sickness absence

The employer should consider, in light of the DDA, discounting disability-related absences when looking at disciplinary procedures, appraisals, references, or selection criteria for redundancy or promotion.

The employer should be prepared to reassess past recorded absences if an employee subsequently discloses that they were disability related. This is particularly important if any disciplinary action against the employee is being considered.

Sickness absence records should, as far as possible, be confidential. However, it may be helpful to discuss with the employee who in the organisation needs to know the reasons for the absences. It may be that only a senior member of the Human Resources team needs to know these reasons. This person can then inform the employee's line manager of any reasonable adjustments that the employee might need without necessarily having to disclose the nature of the disability, if the employee so prefers.

It is likely that using inflexible criteria when considering sickness absences for employment decisions will be discriminatory. For example, a policy that states that if an employee has more days off sick than a specified number then they will not be considered for promotion may well be found to be discriminatory by an Employment Tribunal.

1.5

Cox v The Post Office

This case was important in showing how sickness absence should be recorded and used.

The Post Office has procedures to deal with absenteeism. Mr Cox went through this procedure and was eventually dismissed. However, although disability related absences could be discounted, this did not happen for Mr Cox. The tribunal concluded that but for Mr Cox's asthma related absences he would not have been dismissed and so he had been treated less favourably for a reason relating to his disability. The tribunal also found that the Post Office could have made a reasonable adjustment to review Mr Cox's absence records and disregard disability related absences. That would have prevented dismissal. In concluding that this would have been a reasonable adjustment, the tribunal noted that any cost or disruption would be insignificant considering the size and resources of the Post Office. The tribunal did not accept that the less favourable treatment was justified, there was no indication of disruption to services and the estimated cost of £291 per year was not substantial.

Reasonable adjustments to (and return to) original position

Reasonable adjustments to working arrangements (including the provision of equipment and/or training) or to premises might enable an employee to return to their current post. Disability Employment Advisers (DEAs), contactable through local Jobcentres, carry out workplace assessments and can suggest adjustments that may remove or reduce difficulties that the employee is having in carrying out his or her existing duties because of a disability. DEAs can also provide information about the Access to Work scheme under which employers may be able to claim a contribution towards the cost of making such reasonable adjustments, including equipment, travel costs and personal support.

Knowing that there is a job to go back to can relieve the person's anxiety, aid rehabilitation and thereby enable the employee to return to work more quickly.

Redeployment as an adjustment

If the employee cannot return to their current position the employer needs to consider whether or not they can be transferred to a suitable alternative vacancy. This is a reasonable adjustment under the DDA.

The employer needs to consider both the following questions:

- **is there another position within the organisation to which the employee could be transferred without any reasonable adjustments being made to that post?**

- **is there another position to which the employee could be transferred with reasonable adjustments to that post?**

Remember that reasonable adjustments, which the employer needs to consider to the new position, include:

- **equipment**
- **retraining, to help the person:**
  - **acquire new or different skills**
  - **learn new systems**
- **training to use equipment being used as an adjustment, for example voice recognition software**
- **allocating, to someone else, the non-essential parts of the new job which the employee cannot do because of their disability**
- **working part-time, perhaps as part of a job share (in the case of Wilding v British Telecom, the tribunal found that although BT had made many adjustments, they did not consider part-time work for Mr Wilding)**
- **working flexible hours or from home**
- **time off work to attend a medical appointment.**

Redeployment procedures should be flexible where disabled employees are concerned. Each situation should be treated individually and in a practical manner. Employers will in particular need to reconsider blanket redeployment policies that may have been in place for all employees, regardless of need or disability. These policies may now be discriminatory.

Employers must take active steps to find suitable alternative posts for the employee. It was held in Ridley v NHS Trust that it is not enough for the employer to send the employee vacancy bulletins and suggest that they apply for suitable posts. Nor is it sufficient for an employer simply to ask other departments if they have a vacancy for someone who is currently on long-term sickness absence and cannot return to their original post.

An employer is under no obligation, under the DDA, to create a new job for someone who cannot return to their original position, or be redeployed, after reasonable adjustments have been considered.

London Borough of Hillingdon v Morgan

This case illustrates that redeployment should be considered as well as a gradual return to work for a disabled employee who has been off sick.

Ms Morgan was off sick due to ME. The employer's medical adviser recommended that she should have 'a gradual return to work' and that a

1.5

period of part-time work would ease her back into the routine. Departmental heads within the council, however, decided that there was no suitable work for her and so she was dismissed.

The tribunal found that Hillingdon had discriminated against her by treating her less favourably than some other employees who had been allowed to work from home or had been redeployed. The tribunal did not accept that there was no work for her in such a big organisation, nor that the employer could not enable her to make a graded return to work. The tribunal said that after a month or two the applicant would have been ready for any of the jobs available through Hillingdon's redeployment scheme.

The tribunal also commented that treating the employee as any other employee who was considered for redeployment was wrong. Hillingdon should have tried to make reasonable adjustments so that the disabled employee could be retained in employment.

Arboshe v East London Bus & Coach Co Ltd

This case illustrates what might be suitable alternative vacancies for an employee who has to be redeployed for health and safety reasons. Mr. Arbsohe was a night bus driver, but had his licence withdrawn after being diagnosed with insulin dependent diabetes. He was offered a clerical post or a job as a bus conductor which had a lower salary than his salary as a bus driver. He thought his linguistic skills were not good enough for the clerical post, and although he had the necessary skills to be a bus conductor he did not feel well enough to carry out a conductor's duties.

The company again offered the position of bus conductor to Mr. Arboshe as he had said that he would be willing to consider the post. However, he did not take the post and so his contract was terminated.

The Employment Appeal Tribunal (EAT) decided that although he had been treated less favourably for a reason related to his disability, this was justified. His condition meant that he would lose his licence and the employer had offered him two other positions – 'Had Mr. Arboshe taken the job as a bus conductor there would have been no disability discrimination (and for that matter, no dismissal)'.

In this case, the tribunal found that the bus conductor's job was a suitable alternative vacancy even though it entailed a cut in salary.

This may not be reasonable in every case. It depends on individual facts, such as the size and resources of the employer or extent of pay decrease.

It is important to remember however, that an alternative vacancy which involves a substantial loss of salary or status for the employee may not be considered reasonable, especially if it is possible for the employer to maintain the employee's salary or status.

Return to work interview

Return to work interviews are critical tools in managing sickness absence. When the employee has a definite return date, there should be a return to work interview. This ought to be used to welcome the employee back, provide an update on work issues and discuss any reasonable adjustments. Employers should ensure managers are aware that return to work interviews are not recorded as a disciplinary or incapacity procedure. A return to work interview should not be seen, nor recorded, as a disciplinary procedure.

Termination of contract

An employer may decide in some instances that it has no option but to terminate the employee's contract. Before doing so, the employer should ensure that good practice procedures and all possible reasonable adjustments under the DDA have been considered which could have possibly enabled the person to continue to work for the employer.

The Government's Code of Practice states that dismissal under the DDA 'including compulsory early retirement – of a disabled person for a reason relating to the disability would need to be justified and the reason for it would have to be one which could not be removed by any reasonable adjustment' (Code of Practice for the elimination of discrimination in the field of employment against disabled persons or persons who have a disability, 6.21). The employer should always consult its legal advisers before terminating an employee's contract.

Three distinct types of sickness absence

The following procedures should be used as a guide. Before using them, managers should check their own company guidance to see if procedures are already in place. Procedures may need to be reviewed in light of the DDA.

1 Long term sickness absence – known length

An employee is off work for a set period of time, for example, waiting for, or recuperating from an operation. As the length of sickness absence is known, the organisation could recruit a temporary replacement or temporarily reallocate duties within the team. Whilst the employee is absent, contact should be maintained and the employee kept up to date with developments within the organisation. Allowing an employee to be absent during working hours for rehabilitation, assessment or treatment is given as an example of a reasonable adjustment that employers may have to make in the Code of Practice. These absences are relatively easy to manage, given that they can be planned with the employee beforehand.

Procedure

a **The employee returns to his or her job after a set period of time with or without reasonable adjustments discussed with the employee.**

1.5 b **The employee returns to work in an alternative position. This redeployment could be with or without reasonable adjustments discussed with the employee.**

c **If the employee needs medical treatment, or a second opinion, it may be beneficial for the company to pay for this under a private healthcare scheme rather than the person waiting for treatment on the NHS. This may enable the person to return to work sooner, with knowledge of the job still fresh. This could be a more cost-effective solution when the employer takes into account the costs of recruiting temporary staff, recruitment, the loss of revenue/expertise, training costs, etc.**

d **When the employee is due to come back there should be a return to work interview.**

2 Long term sickness absence – unknown length

An employee continues to send in sickness certificates, but is unable to indicate a date for return. The employer could recruit a temporary replacement or temporarily reallocate duties within the team. Whilst the employee is absent, contact should be maintained and the employee kept up to date with developments within the organisation.

Procedure

a **The employer can ask the employee for his or her doctor's report or independent health assessment, to better understand the impact of the condition.**

b **The employee returns to work with or without reasonable adjustments discussed with the employee.**

c **The employee returns to work in an alternative position. This redeployment could be with or without reasonable adjustments discussed with the employee.**

d **The employer manages without the employee whilst they are off sick. The employer will have to decide how long it is able to accept sick notes to give the employee more opportunity to recover.**

In arriving at this decision the employer will need to take into account:

- **whether, and for how long, other staff can cover the employee's workload**

- **disruption caused by employee's absence**

- **whether or not a temporary replacement can be recruited and how much this will cost**

- **the size and the resources of the organisation and so its ability to absorb the cost and disruption**

The length of time the employee has been with the organisation and the level of specialist skills the employee has are factors to consider when deciding how long the employer can manage without that employee. An employer might wait longer for an employee who has a high level of expertise, or many years' experience with the employer, so that his or her abilities and the employer's investment in that employee are not lost to the organisation.

e **When the employee is due to come back there should be a return to work interview.**

f **If the employee is unable to return to work at all, the employer may decide that it has no option but to terminate the employee's contract. If the employee has a pension scheme – held independently or company-led – the employer could discuss the possibility of early ill health retirement. In addition, if the employer has private health insurance – held independently or company-led – they may be able to make a claim and this should also be discussed. Before taking this step the employer needs to consult its legal advisers.**

3 Periodic sickness absence

There are two kinds of periodic sickness absence:

- **predictable absences**

- **unpredictable absences**

1.5

Predictable short-term absences

Some employees may need to have time off every week, every few weeks, every few months or each year, for example for hospital treatment or counselling. These are reasonable adjustments mentioned in the DDA Code of Practice

Procedure

a **The employee returns to work after a set period of time with or without reasonable adjustments being required as discussed with the employee. Reasonable adjustments can reduce absences. For example, someone with back pain may need time off for back treatment, but an adapted chair or a job that does not put as much strain on the back may mean that the employee does not need as much time off work for treatment.**

b **The employee returns to work in an alternative position. This redeployment could be with or without reasonable adjustments as discussed with the employee. Redeployment may be necessary if the nature of the employee's original job means that regular absences during working hours cannot be accommodated.**

c **When the employee is due to come back there should be a return to work interview, unless the absences are very short.**

1.5

d **If the employer does not think it can keep the job open for the employee or find a reasonable alternative vacancy, it may decide that it has no option but to terminate the employee's contract. If the employee has a pension scheme – held independently or company-led – the employer could discuss the possibility of early ill health retirement. In addition, if the employer has private health insurance – held independently or company-led – they may be able to make a claim and this should also be discussed. Before taking this step the employer needs to consult its legal advisers.**

Unpredictable short-term absences

These absences should flag up that there is an issue that needs investigating, which may or may not be disability related. The employee may not be fully aware of an impairment (e.g. early onset of diabetes) or there maybe other issues. For example, there may be addiction or family problems which the employer needs to be aware of because of the impact on the emplyees' work. Flexibility is crucial when dealing with sickness absences that are short, but unpredictable.

Procedure

a **After a high level of absenteeism has been identified the employer should arrange a meeting to discuss why the employee has been absent so often. The employer should look out for any underlying illness or disability. The absences could relate to:**

- **an existing but previously undisclosed condition that has deteriorated or needs new controlling treatment**
- **a newly diagnosed disability with which the employee is trying to come to terms**
- **an ,as yet, undiagnosed disability but symptoms that are being investigated**
- **a health related condition that could lead to a disability, e.g. RSI discomfort**
- **a non-disability and non-health related issue.**

b **The employer should consider whether any reasonable adjustments need to be made, as discussed with**

the employee. These could include:

– providing equipment or altering working arrangements as the workplace may be aggravating the condition and so contributing to the level of absences

– providing training for the employee. The employee's absences may be stress related, due to the volume or nature of the work. Training may help the employee to better manage their workload and time

– reallocating, temporarily or permanently, some of the employee's duties to other people. These could be duties that are urgent and cannot wait until the employee returns to work

– transferring the employee to a suitable alternative vacancy. A suitable alternative may be one where the employee's unpredictable absences may be more easily accommodated. Additional reasonable adjustments to the alternative job should also be considered

– managing without the employee (whenever the person needs to be absent) by recruiting temporary staff at short notice or providing cover from existing staff. In arriving at this decision the employer will need to consider:

- whether, and for how long, other staff can cover the employee's workload

- the disruption caused by the employee's absence

- whether or not a temporary replacement can be recruited and how much this will cost

- the size and the resources of the organisation and so its ability to absorb the cost and disruption

- the length of service and any specialist skills the employee has should be considered when deciding how the employer can accommodate the absences so that the person's abilities and the employer's investment in the employee are not lost to the organisation

c The employer may think it cannot keep the job open or find a reasonable alternative vacancy. The absences may actually be a straight forward disciplinary matter.

1.5

Therefore, it may decide that it has no option but to terminate the employee's contract. If the employee has a pension scheme – held independently or company-led – the employer could discuss the possibility of early ill health retirement. In addition, if the employer has private health insurance – held independently or company-led – they may be able to make a claim and this should also be discussed. Before taking this step the employer needs to consult its legal advisers.

1.5

Help, advice and information can be obtained from the following organisations

(Contact details are provided at the back of this book).

- **Employers Forum on Disability**
- **The Health and Safety Executive**
- **Jobcentre Plus**
- **Royal National Institute for the Blind**
- **The Society of Occupational Medicine**

A PRACTICAL GUIDE TO

managing recruitment

1.6

Introduction

Under the Disability Discrimination Act it is unlawful for an employer to treat a disabled applicant for a job less favourably than others because of their disability, without justification.
The employer has a duty to make a 'reasonable adjustment' if a disabled applicant is at a substantial disadvantage in relation to others.
The duty applies to all aspects of employment, including recruitment and selection. This paper provides guidance on the sort of adjustments you may need to consider in recruiting people with disabilities. It will help employers to comply with the law, but is principally designed to ensure that what you do reflects best practice, and benefits your business.

How does the DDA define disability?

The term 'disability', as defined by the DDA, refers to any impairment (physical, sensory or mental) with a substantial long-term effect, ie, lasting for more than 12 months. These include for example deafness, blindness, mental health problems, diabetes, dyslexia. Severe disfigurement is also deemed to be disability under the DDA. For more information on the definition of disability see Chapter 1.1 – 'A Brief Introduction to the Disability Discrimination Act'.

Employment facts

In Great Britain there are 8.6 million disabled adults. Of these, 6.9 million are of working age, yet only 3.3 million are in work. Disabled people are five times as likely as non-disabled people to be out of work and claiming benefits.

Employers often regard disabled people as particularly hard to employ. Misconceptions include the belief that people with disabilities are restricted to certain jobs. The truth is that people with disabilities are working in all fields and at all levels. Disabled people have the same employment potential as everyone else. Some, but by no means all, may need adjustments including training and support. All benefit from having a flexible and 'disability competent' employer.

1.6

Another common misconception positions disabled people as a health and safety risk. Research shows however, that disabled people tend to have better attendance records, stay with employers longer and have no more accidents than non-disabled colleagues.

There are other business benefits to becoming disability competent. These include:

- **a larger pool of applicants from which to recruit**
- **enhanced reputation and loyalty from internal and external stakeholders and customers**
- **better understanding of the needs and expectations of disabled people as customers**
- **avoidance of legal action and adverse publicity**
- **increased efficiency linked to staff retention**

How employers are responding

In a move to reduce high turnover of staff within its call centres – and to benefit from a diverse workforce – Centrica initiated a project-led recruitment partnership with Jobcentre Plus (formerly the Employment Service).

Within 6 months of the launch, 50 disabled candidates and carers had been successfully employed on 12-month placement contracts. On follow-up, nearly 90% had progressed to being retained on permanent contracts. Two years on some 150 disabled people have been employed.

Management comment: 'Our new employees are highly motivated and provide a high quality of work. From a wider business perspective, significant benefits have been enjoyed through reduced staff turnover and the creation of a more diverse workforce that better reflects our customer base.'

For further information, see 'Recruitment that Works', available from the Forum.

Reasonable adjustments

It's not just about complying with the law. It makes good business sense to adjust aspects of your business in order to give disabled candidates a fair chance. This may be as detailed as organising a signer three weeks in advance for a deaf candidate; or as broad as challenging preconceived ideas and stereotypes.

Many disabled people represent a significant untapped resource in the labour market and are capable of working once necessary and reasonable adjustments are made. Without such adjustments – and most are simple and inexpensive – good candidates may not apply and their talents is lost. The great majority of disabled people do not require any adjustments – they just need an opportunity to demonstrate what they can do. If, however, you do incur additional costs, grants are available from the government's Access to Work Scheme.

Some of the adjustments suggested for the recruitment and selection of prospective employees, will also be relevant when someone becomes disabled whilst in work.

Job descriptions and candidate specifications

When drawing up job descriptions and candidate specifications:

- **ensure you do not needlessly exclude a disabled candidate**

Example:
Insisting on a handwritten application form, and perfect spelling, may exclude an exceptional candidate who is dyslexic and would otherwise use the computer function 'spell check'.

- **be flexible. Very minor changes can make a significant difference**

Example:
Not taking the time to ensure that job criteria are grouped into what is 'essential' and what is 'desirable', may exclude candidates who are accomplished in the crucial aspects of the role.

- **concentrate on what is to be achieved in a job rather than how it is achieved**

1.6

The following examples show how to allow candidates to demonstrate their capacity to do the job:

'Must touch type.'

This does not explain why touch-typing is essential and may exclude a capable candidate with Repetitive Strain Injury (RSI).

Replace with: 'You will need to produce high quality reports using a word processing package at regular intervals and at short notice'.

This will allow a candidate with RSI to demonstrate their ability to meet the criteria using voice-activated software.

'Must have driving licence.'

This does not explain why a driving licence is essential, and may exclude a candidate with a visual impairment or arthritis who cannot drive.

Replace with 'extensive travel throughout the UK to meet clients is essential'.

The candidate may be able to demonstrate how they will meet this requirement by using alternative methods of transport.

'4 GCSE's required' or 'Work experience required.'

1.6

The first excludes candidates who have not had mainstream education because of their disability. The second excludes candidates who have been discriminated against in the past by employers unwilling to make adjustments.

Replace with 'give examples of how you fulfil the criteria'.

This will allow the candidate to demonstrate any resourcefulness and problem-solving skills which they may have developed either because of their disability or through non work related activities, for example as a parent/governor.

Under the DDA and in terms of organisational effectiveness the outcome is more important than the process. Whenever preparing job descriptions and candidate specifications, keep in mind that a disabled person may carry out the task differently but achieve the same result.

Advertising

When advertising a job, it is important to send the right message to potential candidates:

- **use positive wording like 'we welcome disabled applicants' or 'as members of the Employers' Forum on Disability we are committed to becoming disability confident'**

- **provide a point of contact for people who are concerned about the recruitment process**

- **state that applications will be accepted in alternative formats e.g. on disc, tape or by email**

- **display or mention the disability symbol on written or verbal advertisements if you are a disability symbol holder**

Developed by Jobcentre Plus, the disability symbol (also known as the 2 tick symbol) must be used on every advertisement by symbol holders. It communicates a commitment to best practice – and requires you to interview every disabled applicant who meets the minimum criteria for a vacancy, and to consider them on their abilities.

- **consider advertising in more than one medium. In addition to mainstream press, advertise on local radio, talking newspapers and through the web (assuming your website is accessible)**

- **consider initiating targeted advertising through specialist magazines like Disability Now, websites such as www.jobability.com or employment agencies such as Jobcentre Plus. A factsheet on proactive advertising is available from the Forum**

Application forms

When providing application forms, it is important to reinforce that the organisation wants to encourage disabled people to apply.

- **avoid asking the question: 'Do you have a disability?'**

A candidate may not want to disclose their disability for a variety of reasons.

State instead: 'You will be asked at a later stage if you need us to make any adjustments for the interview. If you wish to discuss any concerns about the application process, please contact....' This shows a willingness to make reasonable adjustments at every stage of the recruitment process.

- **avoid stipulating how the application form should be completed**

Be prepared to accept application forms or CVs in alternative formats, for example audiotape, disk or e-mail.

If the applicant can apply in a variety of formats, it may be reasonable to specify the one you would prefer to receive and will respond in, for example, e-mail rather than Braille.

Website applications

The worldwide web has the potential to offer disabled people unparalleled opportunities to interact and contribute their experiences, skills and purchasing power. While the use of the Internet in finding and placing candidates is increasing rapidly, website accessibility is yet to become a norm.

Responsible employers are now becoming aware of their duty as service providers under Part III of the DDA to make their websites accessible to disabled people – and acting on it. Any candidate disadvantaged by an inaccessible e-recruitment process may also have a claim under Part II of the DDA.

- **if you are advertising through the web, check to see how accessible your, or your agency's, website is**

- **the Bobby Worldwide program www.cast.org/bobby can be accessed directly to examine a website page-by-page or downloaded to examine a website thoroughly – and should be used as part of a more comprehensive audit (Contact the Forum for details of our web audit service)**

- **The Forum publication 'Accessible Website Design' will also enable you to deliver website accessibility for people with a diverse range of disabilities**

Employment Agencies: The Staffing Industry

Employment or recruitment agencies, as service providers, have an obligation not to treat disabled people less favourably than others. This includes making reasonable changes to their practices, policies or procedures when these make it impossible or unreasonably difficult for disabled people to use the service.

1.6

Employment agencies are also increasingly being asked by their clients to demonstrate disability competence and commitment to best practice given that failure to do so may render their clients liable under the DDA.
An agency may have to:

- **provide auxiliary aids or services. Examples include providing sign language interpreters and/or a text phone for a deaf candidate; or providing information in alternative formats such as large print or audiotape for candidates with a visual impairment**

- **offer an interview at an alternative accessible venue if physical features of the original interview venue make it difficult to access**

- **in the lead-up to October 2004 consider removing or altering physical features of their premises that make it difficult for disabled people to access the service**

It is vital that the employment agency is aware of both the requirements of:

- **part III of the DDA that applies it as a service provider**

- **part II of the DDA that applies to it as an agent for its client**

The agency must also be aware of its client's commitment to employing a diverse workforce through best practice recruitment.

If an agency does your short-listing interviews, ensure their processes are non-discriminatory. Under the DDA, employers are obliged to ensure that their agency treats all disabled candidates fairly. We would recommend that you build your expectations of how the agency will meet your – and its own – obligations under the DDA into your contract with the agency.

Ask Employment agencies to monitor the number of disabled people they shortlist and interview. If you are a two tick symbol holder ensure that the agency is aware of this and will interview all disabled candidates who meet the minimum criteria for the job.

Shortlisting

When reviewing an application form or CV from a disabled person, it is important to remember:

- **if an applicant seems over-qualified there could be a legitimate disability related reason for a change of career or a seeming backtrack**

- formal education qualifications may not be an accurate indicator of capability as many disabled people have been disadvantaged by the education system

- periods of inactivity may be directly related to disability

- not to discount voluntary work and life experience. Candidates may have gained invaluable organisational and creative problem-solving skills in response to their experience of disability

The recruitment interview

Offer of Interview

Follow-up on your willingness to make adjustments. Let every candidate know you are happy to discuss any adjustments required, irrespective of whether the candidate discloses a disability.

You should:

- offer information about the interview in alternate formats

- ensure a fully accessible interview location. Check, for example, that exits and toilets are wide enough for a wheel chair if your candidate uses one

- ask the candidate if they would prefer to organise a signer or support worker if one is needed or if you should do so. Make it clear that you will pay for the service regardless of who organises it. Allow for at least three weeks to arrange a signer

- be prepared to offer the candidate the alternative of a single interviewer (with an observer present), rather than an interviewing panel. This may be especially helpful for example for someone whose stammer increases under pressure

- become disability-confident as an employer. Reading the Forum's Disability Communication Guide will help. Understand that no two people experience disability in the same way. Be open to learning

- involve every member of staff in disability awareness and equality training including the reception desk and security

- consider offering alternatives to the standard interview. A candidate who has a speech impediment, for example, may prefer to be interviewed by text phone, email or in person. Some candidates may benefit from job tryouts if their disability makes it difficult for them to convey their potential at a standard interview

- guarantee interviews for disabled candidates who meet the minimum criteria – and keep those criteria truly "minimum"

- find out more. The Forum has a Helpline for its members and can

answer questions about any stage of the recruitment process. Contact the Forum helpline on 020 7403 3020

Whilst particular adjustments may be needed, for many disabled candidates all that will be required is an open mind on the part of the potential employer.

Legal Case Study

Murphy v Sheffield Hallam University

1.6

Mr Murphy applied for the job of Learner Support Co-ordinator. In his application Mr Murphy said that he was profoundly deaf. The tribunal noted that that this would have put the employer on notice that a sign language interpreter would be required for the interview. However, the requirement for a sign language interpreter was not considered until two weeks after Mr Murphy's application form was received and eight days before the interview. The University did make some efforts to obtain a sign language interpreter before the interview but these failed and were in the tribunal's findings `late and inadequate`.

When Mr Murphy arrived at the interview he discovered that no sign interpreter had been provided. Some pressure was put on Mr Murphy to continue with the interview relying on lip-reading or writing. However, after an initial attempt he refused to proceed and the interview was adjourned for a week. Hallam University asked Mr Murphy to provide his own sign language interpreter at their expense. The tribunal noted that this was not a reasonable attitude because with their resources it would have been easier for them to find someone or, if they could not, to adjourn the interview until a date when they could.

The interview took place with a competent amateur sign language interpreter. Mr Murphy was not appointed, a hearing person got the job. Mr Murphy argued that this was as a result of the inadequate arrangements made for the interview and the university's fears about the costs of providing him with reasonable adjustments in the job.

The tribunal found in his favour regarding the discriminatory interview arrangements, but did not consider that he had proved that he'd been discriminated against with regard to the actual appointment to the job. They awarded him £2,500 for injury to feelings.

Pre employment tests

Psychometric test

Psychometric tests can help determine an individual's abilities and potential.

However the DDA places a duty on employers to make reasonable adjustments to any tests to ensure that they are fair.

Consult the issuer of the test on how flexible it can be and what adjustments can be made for disabled candidates without invalidating the results.

Ability tests

If selection involves a technical or other test of ability to carry out the job tasks, be sure that it does not discriminate.

Employers may need to do one or more of the following:

- **ensure the test is designed to assess only the essential components of the job**
- **change the format of the test, for example, from written into audio, or from small into large print**
- **allow written tests to be done on a computer and adapt software, voice output etc. where appropriate**
- **allow for the presence of a support worker**
- **weight the total score to take into account questions that the applicant identifies as problematic as a result of their disability**
- **apply a more qualitative and flexible approach to scoring. Comparisons with the 'norm' may be neither accurate nor useful**
- **ensure the venue and work station is accessible e.g. a large monitor screen might be needed for a particular candidate**
- **be flexible with time. A candidate may, for example, need to stand or walk around to alleviate back pain or write slowly because of their disability**
- **a practice test can be sent to the candidate prior to interview so that the candidate can specify adjustments needed. This will also reassure a disabled candidate who fears an inaccessible test**

Remember that the purpose of the test is to assess every candidate's ability to do the job. Reasonable adjustments for a disabled candidate should only ensure that the candidate has the opportunity to demonstrate their capabilities on a level playing field with everyone else. It is not reasonable to adjust the test in favour of the disabled candidate to the extent that they cannot demonstrate that they can carry out the job tasks to the standard required.

Group Assessment/Assessment Centres are sometimes used to measure teamwork and leadership skills and can be inherently problematic for many disabled candidates if the groups and tasks are not disability aware. Be aware that if assessment is in groups, particular adjustments may be required. For example, if one of the candidates is deaf, a visual indicator may be needed to inform candidates that only one person should speak at a time. Scoring may then need to take into account different group dynamics. Take expert advice for candidates who can be (and often are) significantly disadvantaged by being forced to work in a new deaf unaware team as part of the assessment process.

Interview questions

1.6

Avoid asking for medical details and personal questions as to how the disability was acquired. All that is needed at this stage is to understand how the disability affects the candidate in the workplace.

- **questions should focus on the key competencies needed for the position, not on the person's disability**

- **make it clear life experience and voluntary work will be considered when asking a candidate to demonstrate their ability to fulfil criteria for the role**

- **ensure questions focus on 'out-put' – the desired end result**

- **if the job demands certain physical and/or mental tasks, be as specific as possible. For example, if lifting is involved, refer to the exact weight and how often it will be necessary**

- **towards the end of the interview, ask every applicant if any reasonable adjustments need to be provided to help them do the job. This encompasses disability-related adjustments, and also allows for further discussion on other general adjustments. For instance, a candidate may need to start earlier or later because of caring commitments**

Health examinations

Only ask a disabled candidate to complete a health questionairre or to undergo a medical check-up if it is your policy to require this of every candidate. Singling out disabled candidates for a health check is likely to be discriminatory.

If a health examination is required, ensure that every question clearly relates to the work criteria for every candidate. If a history of sickness absence is required, ensure sickness rates are differentiated into disability and non-disability related absences. It may be discriminatory to reject a disabled candidate because they had high levels of sickness absence related to their disability in a previous job.

Remember that medical history or past sickness absence levels cannot successfully predict future work performance. The candidate may now be managing that disability better or the absences could have related to a former employer's unwillingness to make reasonable adjustments.

Chapter 1.5 – 'Managing Sickness Absence' and Chapter 1.3 – 'Disability Management and the Medical Advisor' outline good practice in using medical information.

The job offer

For many reasons, applicants may not have declared a hidden disability such as diabetes or a mental health problem during the recruitment process.

Many people do not regard their impairment to be a disability. Some are unwilling to disclose this sort of information for fear of being discriminated against. Others feel that their disability has no bearing on their capacity to do the job they are applying for and so is irrelevant.

When offering the job, give every candidate another opportunity to discuss any adjustments they may require.

The best person to advise on reasonable adjustments is usually the applicant; however do not assume everyone knows every adjustment that might be helpful. Remember that the candidate may also be concerned that the cost of adjustments may discourage the employer from offering them the job.

You should ensure that the candidate is aware that most employers can apply for a grant for reasonable adjustments through Access to Work.

Job offers are sometimes conditional on adjustments being in place by a particular time. This allows time to investigate adjustments and possible funding from, for example, Access to Work.

In exceptional cases it may be unreasonable – due to time and cost – to implement the adjustments, and there may be no other option but to withdraw the offer. This could, for example, be if there is an urgent need to fill a short-term temporary post quickly. This might be deemed to be a material and substantial reasons under the DDA and so the withdrawal of the offer might be justified. However, exploring all options and coming to interim arrangements is to be preferred and recommended.

Monitoring the recruitment process

Monitoring how many disabled people apply for the position enables an organisation to review its recruitment policies and procedures so as to avoid unintentionally limiting opportunities for disabled people.

Help, advice and information can be obtained from the following organisations

(Contact details are provided at the back of this book).

- **Employers Forum on Disability**
- **Saville and Holdsworth**
- **The Royal National Institute for the Blind (RNIB)**
- **Disability Rights Commission**
- **Jobcentre Plus: (formerly known as The Employment Service)**
- **AbilityNet**

employers' forum on disability

Sponsored by

UNUMPROVIDENT℠

Chapter two

Practical Adjustments

A PRACTICAL GUIDE TO

employment adjustments for people with visual impairments

Employment facts

Adjustments in recruitment and selection

Adjustments in employment

2.7

Introduction

Under the Disability Discrimination Act it is unlawful for an employer to treat a disabled applicant or employee less favourably than others because of their disability.

The employer has a duty to make a 'reasonable adjustment' if a disabled applicant or employee is at a substantial disadvantage in relation to others. The duty applies both to physical features of the employer's premises, e.g. buildings, fittings and equipment, and to all aspects of employment and employment practices, including recruitment and selection, training, transfer, career development and retention.

It is good business sense to make adjustments. Visually impaired people represent a significant untapped resource in the labour market and at work their talents are often under-utilised. Most visually impaired people would be capable of working if adjustments – which may very well be simple and inexpensive – were made. Without such adjustments, good candidates may not apply and good employees may be lost.

This section provides guidance on the sort of adjustments you may want to consider in recruiting and employing visually impaired people. Those suggested at recruitment, for example in meeting, greeting and communicating with people with visual impairments, may also be relevant in the work situation. The concluding part of this section provides details of further sources of information, expert advice and help.

What is visual impairment?

The term 'visually impaired' refers to people who are blind or partially sighted.

Each person with impaired vision is different. Not only is the degree and nature of the impairment particular to the individual, ability and expectations naturally vary too.

Employment facts

2.7

In the United Kingdom there are one million visually impaired people, 90,000 of working age. Yet of those 90,000 only 22,000, i.e. approximately one in four are in work.

Employers often regard people with sight problems as particularly hard to employ. Misconceptions include the belief that people with visual impairments are restricted to certain jobs, such as telephone operating, and that they cannot work with computers. Of those in work, 75% are doing the same job they were doing when they developed sight problems; thus most jobs can be undertaken by visually impaired people. With training and support visually impaired people have demonstrated the same employment potential as anyone else.

Contrary to popular myth, visually impaired people are not a safety risk. In fact, because of their disability they tend to be more safety-conscious than sighted colleagues.

Job descriptions and candidate specifications

When drawing up job descriptions and candidate specifications:

- **do not needlessly exclude a visually impaired candidate. For example, is a requirement to drive essential, or are there alternative methods of getting around?**
- **be flexible. Concentrate on what is to be achieved in a job rather than on how it is achieved. A visually impaired person may do things differently**

Equipment

Stuart Foster, a senior analyst programmer with BT, is blind. His PC is adapted to convert his screen work to speech, which allows him to access mainframes, e-mail and Microsoft products. He tapes his meetings and takes notes in braille. Approximate costs: synthesised speech output £300, software for access to 'Windows' £450, brailler £200 - total £950 approx., borne by BT.

Management comment: "Stuart has been with BT for 16 years and performs to the highest standards. The cost of his equipment is very worthwhile, considering his value to us as an employee".

Advertising

When advertising a job:

- **encourage visually impaired people to apply by including a statement in the advertisement about your commitment to equal opportunity**

- **consider the print size and type used in the advertisement. 12 point is the recommended minimum for accessibility. Avoid light type weights and unusual type faces. The Employers' Forum Customer Action File No.2 – Producing Accessible Information, includes guidelines on ensuring your literature is accessible**

- **consider local radio, talking newspapers, organisations for visually impaired people**

- **consult the Disability Service Team based at your local Jobcentre**

Application forms

An application form can be the first barrier facing a suitably qualified and experienced candidate:

- **use a simple, clear type face**

- **where possible, use matt, pastel-coloured paper**

- **be ready to provide the form and job details in large print, braille, on tape or on disk. Better still, offer this facility when the job is advertised. (Remember that 60% of all blind and partially-sighted people in the UK regard themselves as print readers. Only a few people will require braille)**

- **make it clear that a signature is not required if a tape is used**

Ability tests

If selection normally involves a test, be sure that it does not discriminate against a visually impaired person:

- **discuss the testing with the test publisher and seek guidance on possible adjustments including alternative formats**

- **consult visually impaired candidates in advance so that necessary adjustments can be made, eg providing a text enlarger on the computer monitor, or allowing the test to be completed orally instead of in writing**

- **ensure that test instructions are clearly read aloud**

- **allow more time for candidates using magnification aids or braille**

- **be prepared to waive the test. There are often other equally satisfactory ways of getting the information**

Saville and Holdsworth have produced 'Guidelines For Testing People With Disabilities' and have a helpline. RNIB have produced 'Psychometric testing and visual impairment'.

The recruitment interview

You need to know whether, with a 'reasonable adjustment', your visually impaired applicant is the best person for the job.

- **consider how the candidate will reach the interview venue. If public transport could prove difficult, offer to reimburse the taxi fare**
- **prepare the layout of the interview room so the candidate can get around**
- **ensure that reception and security staff know how to welcome and assist visually impaired visitors**
- **ask if the candidate wishes to be accompanied from reception to the interview. If so, offer an arm and guide the person to the chair. If your offer is declined, lead the way at a steady pace and continue talking**
- **ensure that, if possible, interviewers do not sit with a light source directly behind them. They should introduce themselves clearly, giving the candidate time to relax and to identify panel members**
- **focus on the person's capacity to do the job – with or without an adjustment – not on the visual impairment. If you have any doubts about a person's ability to do the job simply ask them how they would go about it**

Remember that the Employment Service's (Job Centre Plus) Access to Work programme can part-fund adaptations to equipment, a personal reader and the costs incurred in getting to and from work.

Induction and training

How accessible is your standard induction and training programme? You may need to consider:

- **allowing more time and greater flexibility for induction and training**
- **allowing the employee to organise their work area**
- **assigning a colleague to help the employee find their way around the work area**
- **ensuring that training material and job instructions are available in the appropriate format, e.g. large print, braille, on tape, disk or email**
- **avoiding red ink on flip charts in training sessions**

Start getting the adjustments in place as soon as practicable after you have made an appointment – it may take time.

Before the employee starts work, ensure that:

- **their manager or supervisor understands the agreed adjustments**

- **the workgroup is briefed on the adjustments and on basic 'disability communication'**

Training

Peter White, who is blind, was engaged by the BBC as Disability Affairs Correspondent. The Access to Work programme provided him with a special computer, a scanner and braille embosser which enable him both to access and produce print. He received four days training to familiarise him with the equipment. The BBC then arranged a week's training in how to derive full benefit from the equipment and in how to access the BBC's main computerised database. Management comment: "The week's training has considerably enlarged the scope of Peter's job – to our mutual benefit."

Doing the job

Consult your visually impaired employees. They're usually the experts on how best to manage the effects of their disability at work. Adjustments may cost little or nothing, for example:

- **a dot of silicon on a knob, switch or button enables an operator to align controls on a machine**
- **a wide felt-tip marker may make file folder labels readable**
- **tactile indicators on the underside of stair-rails denote the floor level**
- **a colleague can regularly set a little time aside to read mail for a visually impaired person. It may be possible to get a support worker under the Access to Work scheme**

Numerous high-tech aids are available. Some examples of how computers can be modified are:

- **magnification systems enlarge the size of the text or graphics on the screen**
- **synthetic speech systems read out the information on a screen**
- **electronic braille displays enable a visually impaired person to 'read' the screen via a strip of electronically controlled pins connected to the computer**

In addition, there are devices that enable a visually impaired person to read printed material:

- **closed circuit televisions (CCTVs) magnify printed material and enable a person with useable vision to read documents**
- **optical character recognition (OCR) systems, also known as 'reading machines', scan printed material and transfer it to a connected personal computer where it can be read by a speech or braille system**

Career development

Visually impaired people will have the same career aspirations and ambitions as other employees:

- **appraise and promote them using the same criteria as for others**
- **provide the same opportunities for learning and for new challenges - consult them about what adjustments are necessary**
- **deal with performance problems openly and do not assume they are disability-related**

2.7

Retention

Employees who develop a sight problem which begins to affect their competence are often unwilling or unable to admit, sometimes even to themselves, the seriousness of what is happening. It may be helpful to build into your annual appraisal system a mechanism for identifying and resolving disability-related problems.

It is usually in your interest to retain an employee who develops a disability. Skills and experience are not lost. The employer saves the cost of recruiting and training a replacement, and possibly the cost of early retirement.

Transfer to other work

A cable layer employed by Northern Electric contracted an eye disease which affected his vision so that he could no longer do the job safely. After a four week assessment and rehabilitation course organised by the Employment Service (Job Centre Plus) he was transferred to engineering services as a clerical assistant, where, with the help of a large screen reader and a CCTV, he did work involving reading engineering documents and drawings. The equipment was provided under Access to Work. Three years later he was transferred to office services where his duties include reception, switchboard operation and mail.

Management comment: "Phil has demonstrated that with readiness to adapt on his part, and with the help of equipment, a radical change of job is possible. His transfer sent a positive message to other employees."

Help, advice and information can be obtained from the following organisations

(Contact details are provided at the back of this book).

- **AbilityNet**
- **Employers' Forum on Disability**
- **Jobcentre Plus**
- **The Royal National Institute for the Blind (RNIB)**
- **Saville and Holdsworth**

A PRACTICAL GUIDE TO

employment adjustments for deaf or hard of hearing people

Working effectively with a deaf or hard of hearing person

Adjustments in recruitment and selection

Adjustments in employment

2.8

Introduction

Under the Disability Discrimination Act (DDA) (1995), it is unlawful for an employer to treat a disabled applicant for a job, or an employee, less favourably, without justification. An employer also has a duty under the DDA to make reasonable adjustments to prevent a disabled employee from being placed at a substantial disadvantage by any physical feature of the premises, or by working arrangements. The duty applies to all aspects of employment, including recruitment and selection, training, transfer, career development and retention.

The DDA defines a disabled person as someone who has, or had, "a physical or mental impairment, which has a substantial and long-term adverse effect" on their ability to carry out normal day-to-day activities. "Long-term" means that it must have lasted, or be expected to last, at least 12 months.

Anyone with a substantial long-term hearing loss is covered by the Act. This includes people who have difficulty following speech without a hearing aid, whether or not they actually use a hearing aid.

This paper provides guidance on the sort of adjustments you may need to consider in recruiting and employing deaf or hard of hearing people. It also tells you where to obtain further help, expert advice and information.

The term 'deaf' tends to refer to people who have a profound or severe hearing loss. The term 'Hard of hearing' tends to refer to people who have a mild to severe hearing loss.

Employment facts

Training/equipment/support

Jeremy Irwin, who is profoundly deaf, joined the Department of Social Security as a 'fast stream' graduate trainee in October 1996. The Department have provided him with a textphone, a vibrating pager and a Typetalk account and he has access to lipspeakers to enable him to participate in Departmental and Civil Service College training courses.

2.8

According to the Labour Force Survey, people who are deaf or hard of hearing are twice as likely to be unemployed as people in general. Those in work are more likely to be in semi-skilled or unskilled jobs than others in work. Yet there are very few jobs which deaf or hard of hearing people cannot do, given training and workplace adjustments.

Adjustments may very well be simple and inexpensive and they make good business sense. Without adjustments, good candidates may not apply for jobs and good employees may be lost. Precise requirements vary from one individual to another. Always ask the deaf or hard of hearing person what they need.

Under Working effectively with a deaf or hard of hearing person

Hard of hearing people

The majority of hard of hearing people have a degree of hearing, often enhanced by a hearing aid. They may rely on lip reading and are likely to benefit from:

- **induction loops, which enable hard of hearing people to tune their hearing aids in directly to speakers at meetings. Other amplification options include FM and infra red systems**
- **lip speakers, who soundlessly repeat what is being said, using clear lip patterns**
- **telephones with controllable amplification.**

Reallocation of duties/equipment

After working for the Halifax for nearly 20 years, Margaret Hoyes, a customer services assistant, had an illness which resulted in severe deafness. She had five months sickness absence on full pay, after which the Halifax made some adjustments to her duties to enable her to return to her former job. With help from Access to Work two telephones were fitted with an amplification device for Margaret's use. She was also issued with programmable hearing aids and a

'conference folder', which provides amplification at meetings.

Deaf people

Deaf people may rely mainly on lip reading, and also use a hearing aid, but may benefit from one or more of the following:

- **lip speakers to assist lip reading**
- **simultaneous speech-to-text transcriptions, for example using Palantype (a computer-based system which allows a trained operator, through a special keyboard, to produce verbatim text on a speech at the speed of ordinary speech)**
- **a note-taker to make a record of what has been said**
- **sign language interpreters**
- **subtitles on videos, eg training videos**

Deaf people may also need a textphone. This comprises a keyboard and a small screen which allows the user to access the telephone network, either directly using or via Textdirect or Typetalk (the national relay service which enables deaf, hard of hearing, deafened and speech-impaired people to communicate with hearing people).

Deaf people may also use the visual languages British Sign Language (BSL), or Sign Supported English (SSE). SSE is a combination of signs from BSL used with English grammar. Some deaf people's first language may be BSL and English their second language.

Deaf people may need sign language interpreters at meetings and conferences. Due to the shortage of interpreters, the interpreter needs to be booked between 4-6 weeks in advance.

Technology

Advances in technology are continually improving the work opportunities for deaf or hard of hearing people.
For example:

- **Hi-linc and similar video systems for captioning live or pre-recorded programmes to enable deaf people to take part in spoken meetings and conversations at work. It is extremely easy to use and can be operated using a minimum of keyboard skills**
- **portable loops are available for use at conferences**
- **SMS on mobile phones, email and fax machines are particularly useful**
- **video telephones and PC-based videotelephony**

Sign Language Interpreter

The Natural History Museum employs in the Library and Information Services Department a cataloguer who is deaf. The Museum engages a sign language interpreter to enable her to participate in monthly departmental meetings and local team briefings and to attend corporate meetings. Before meetings the interpreter is given a copy of the handout or brief so that she can familiarise herself with any technical points. Access to Work refunds 80% of the costs of the interpreter.

Reasonable adjustments – recruitment

2.8 You need to make sure you do not discriminate against a disabled job applicant during the recruitment procedure. You may also have to make reasonable adjustments. It is important not to make assumptions about what the applicant can or cannot do. Instead, ask applicants about reasonable adjustments as part of the recruitment procedure.

When drawing up job descriptions and candidate specifications:

- **make sure they are not vague**
- **be flexible. Very often minor changes can make a significant difference**
- **concentrate on what is to be achieved in a job rather than how it is achieved. A deaf or hard of hearing person may simply do things differently, for example, communicate externally using email, in writing, or using Typetalk or Textdirect.**

When advertising a job:

- **encourage deaf or hard of hearing to apply by including a statement about your commitment to equal opportunities**
- **consult your local Disability Service Team through the Employment Service**
- **consider advertising in magazines such as British Deaf News, using the special information pages for deaf viewers on Teletext (BBC2 P.640), and through local deaf clubs**
- **make contact with deaf organisations, such as The Royal National Institute for Deaf People (RNID) who have an employment unit**
- **consider advertising on the internet, for example The Royal Association for Deaf People's website www.royaldeaf.org.uk**

Interviews and tests

Before the interview or test, establish the person's communication needs, for example, does the candidate require a loop system or radio hearing aid or a sign language interpreter. Due to the shortage of interpreters, the interpreter needs to be booked between 4-6 weeks in advance.

As you want to recruit the best person for the job, you should ensure you focus on the person's capacity to do the job, not on the person's deafness or hearing loss. After discussing the person's skills and abilities for the job, you should establish with the candidate whether, to fulfil the key requirements of the job, any equipment or other adjustments would be necessary.

Remember that that the Employment Service's Access to Work programme can provide help with the extra costs of recruiting and employing deaf or hard of hearing people, including the services of sign language interpreters or note-takers, or equipment such as textphones or electronic alerting devices.

If selection involves a test:

- **information or instructions normally presented orally may need to be given in writing, or through a sign language interpreter or lipspeaker**
- **the verbal content of a test may be discriminatory if it is not directly applicable to a job**
- **provide comprehensive written instructions and ensure they are understood**
- **allow extra time for explanation of the test requirements and administration**

At the interview:

- **allow the candidate time to adjust to unfamiliar lip patterns and tune-in to the interviewer(s)**
- **position yourself so that light falls on your face. It is almost impossible for someone to lipread if the speaker is in front of a window, because of the glare**
- **look directly at the interviewee, maintaining eye contact**
- **don't cover your mouth**
- **don't shout - just speak a little more slowly and distinctly**
- **be patient if not immediately understood. Rephrase what you said rather than just repeating yourself. Some people have difficulty in lipreading certain words**
- **if a sign language interpreter is used in the interview, speak directly to the candidate, not to the interpreter. The interpreter's role is to facilitate communication, not to participate in the interview. Interpreters observe strict confidentiality**

Reasonable adjustments – employment

Deaf awareness

Most deaf people say that what helps them most at work is colleagues who have a basic awareness of deafness and how it affects communication.

Deaf awareness training helps colleagues learn how to make themselves more easily understood, for example where to stand or sit in meetings to ease lipreading, and the importance of passing on key information.

In-house sign language classes may be useful for the team in which the employee works.

2.8

Training

Deaf and hard of hearing employees should have equal access to in-house and external training and career development opportunities. Ask what is required in order to participate fully in training, e.g. a sign language interpreter, a lip speaker, a note-taker, a radio aid or loop system.

Inform course tutors or trainers when they have deaf participants on a programme, and ensure that they know how to make their training accessible. They should:

- **provide handouts, a reading list and written notes introducing any new vocabulary**
- **if possible meet deaf and hard of hearing participants in advance, to determine individual requirements**
- **establish a collaborative relationship with sign language interpreters or lipspeakers and provide course material**
- **arrange for transcripts of any videos, or, if the material is in regular use, get it subtitled**
- **be aware of communication needs (see Interviews and Tests)**

Further adjustments

As well as the adjustments mentioned in the section Working effectively with a deaf or hard of hearing person, further adjustments which cost nothing and may be helpful include:

- **ensuring the office and/or work environment is well lit**
- **locating the employee where environment noise is minimised**
- **arranging the workplace so that the employee can see when someone enters and also so that communication is made easier for the deaf or hard of hearing person to communicate with colleagues and vice-versa**

After the employee has settled in the job ask if other adjustments might be needed or whether adjustments already made need to be reviewed. Ensure that you take the same approach to adjustments when a deaf or hard of hearing person goes for promotion, again not making assumptions about what the employee can or cannot do.

Retaining employees

It is usually in your interest to retain an employee who develops a disability so that skills and experience are not lost. You save the cost of recruiting and training a replacement, and possibly the cost of early retirement.

By regularly talking to employees about their work, for example in appraisals, you may be able to notice difficulties that may be attributable to an employee losing their hearing. This will then give you an opportunity to talk about adjustments that may enable the employee to work more effectively.

Safety

Research has shown that deaf and hard of hearing people have as good a safety record as others, if not better. While the risks are often overestimated, some straightforward precautions are sensible:

- **fire alarms should have flashing lights**

- **machinery with safety alarms can be converted to produce flashing lights**

- **deaf employees must know about emergency exits and fire drills. Sometimes a 'buddy' is assigned to help in an evacuation**

- **a pager with a vibrating signal may be issued to a deaf or hard of hearing employee whose job is itinerant**

- **the emergency button in a lift should have a light showing when it has been activated**

Help, advice and information can be obtained from the following organisations

(Contact details are provided at the back of this book).

- **AbilityNet**
- **British Deaf Association**
- **BT Textdirect**
- **The Council for Advancement of Communication with Deaf People (CACDP)**
- **Employers' Forum on Disability**
- **Disability Rights Commission**
- **Jobcentre Plus**
- **The Royal National Institute for Deaf People (RNID)**
- **RNID Typetalk**
- **Saville and Holdsworth**

A PRACTICAL GUIDE TO

employment adjustments for people with progressive or fluctuating conditions

Equal opportunity policy and training

Adjustments to working arrangements

Disclosure and confidentiality

The role of occupational health specialists

2.9

Introduction

Under the Disability Discrimination Act (DDA) it is unlawful for an employer to treat a disabled applicant or employee less favour-ably than others because of their disability.
The employer has a duty to make a 'reasonable adjustment' if a disabled applicant or employee is at a substantial disadvantage in relation to others. The duty applies both to physical features of the employer's premises, e.g. buildings, fittings and equipment, and to all aspects of employment, including recruitment and selection, training, transfer, career development and retention.

These adjustments aim to give a disabled employee a fair opportunity to be assessed on their true merits rather than in terms of their disability, so they are not disadvantaged compared with non-disabled colleagues.

Definition

The DDA definition of disability covers a broad range of people, some of whom would not normally consider themselves disabled. This will include some people with long-term medical conditions and incorporates two categories. Progressive conditions are those with symptoms which tend to increase in severity over time, while the symptoms of fluctuating conditions will come and go, often at random.

Many people with progressive or fluctuating conditions sometimes experience extensive periods of remission. With most conditions, the onset, progress or decline of symptoms, and the degree of impairment they cause, will vary between individuals. In the majority of cases, these effects and their timescale are impossible to predict with accuracy.

2.9

Disability is generally defined by the DDA as 'a physical or mental impairment which has a substantial and long-term adverse effect' on a person's ability to carry out normal day-to-day activities. 'Long-term' means that it must have lasted, or be expected to last, at least 12 months.

Special rules apply to people with progressive conditions who are covered by the DDA from the moment any impairment resulting from that condition has some effect on their ability to carry out normal day-to-day activities. The effect need not be continuous and need not yet be substantial, providing that eventually it is likely to be substantial. As examples of progressive conditions, the Act cites cancer, HIV infection, multiple sclerosis and muscular dystrophy.

The Government proposes that the definition of disability should be extended to cover people with HIV from the point of diagnosis, and people with cancer from at which it is diagnosed as requiring substantial treatment.

People with fluctuating conditions are also covered if the substantial adverse effects are likely to recur. For example, someone with ME may have an episode lasting a few weeks, and then have a period of remission. Conditions which recur sporadically or for short periods, e.g. back pain, can also qualify.
If it is not clear whether an individual is covered by the Act, it would be prudent to assume that they are covered, and to consider what adjustments are necessary for them to do the job. Perhaps no adjustments are needed, other than a willingness to let them demonstrate their capabilities. Adopting best practice will usually prove more fruitful than a policy of attempting to simply keep within the law, or spending time and money on recruiting a new employee.

Managing effectively

There are three important areas of misunderstanding which often affect the management of people with progressive or fluctuating conditions at work. It is crucial to be aware of these:

'Invisibility'

It is often impossible to tell from someone's appearance that they have a progressive or fluctuating condition, e.g. back pain, mental illness. In the early stages of some conditions, the symptoms may also be so slight they cannot be detected, e.g. Parkinson's Disease, arthritis or multiple sclerosis.

'Confusion with ill health'

Even when it is acknowledged that an individual has a progressive or fluctuating condition, there is a tendency not to regard the person as disabled, but to treat the matter as a health or sickness problem. Indeed, many people with progressive or fluctuating conditions do not regard themselves as disabled and may well regard the term as stigmatising. Because the condition is not viewed as a disability, no thought is given to possible adjustments, which can in turn lead to litigation under the DDA.

'Unwarranted assumptions'

It is important to avoid the tendency to base an assessment of a person's capabilities on the assumption that they will inevitably be unable to work at some point in the future. Accurate prediction of the progress of a person's condition is often impossible and many progressive and fluctuating conditions can be satisfactorily managed over the years through the use of flexible working practices. It is also important not to assume that a person with such a condition will always present problems for an employer. Many conditions are effectively and successfully controlled with medication or other treatments.

Hours / support worker

A ward clerk who has worked at St Thomas' Hospital for 16 years developed severe arthritis, necessitating a long period of sickness absence. She returned to work on reduced hours for six weeks on full pay, before returning to full-time working. Because she uses sticks her workstation has been completely rearranged to facilitate her mobility. The Hospital Trust arranged for a support worker to assist her, for nine hours a week, with the onerous filing duties the job entails. Access to Work covers 80% of the costs.

Recruitment and selection

If you use application forms, you should encourage people to say if they need adjustments at any stage. When people are asked for interview, they must be asked if they need any adjustments. Many people with progressive or fluctuating conditions will not need these.

The DDA does not prevent you from seeking information about a disability, but medical questions should be restricted to those which are relevant to the job. Always be clear why you want the information and how it will be used. The assessment of an individual's fitness for work should be seen as separate from the recruitment process.

Disclosure

Many progressive and fluctuating conditions are not obvious, so the employer has to rely on the employee to make a disclosure. However, employees are often reluctant to do this because they are afraid of experiencing discrimination. This is particularly true for people with conditions which attract prejudice and discrimination, such as HIV or mental health problems.
If applicants and employees know that you have a positive equal opportunity policy, and in particular that there is a willingness to make reasonable adjustments for all disabled applicants and employees, they will be much more inclined to disclose their disability.

Disclosure can be beneficial because:

- **the stress of not divulging a disability may exacerbate the person's difficulties**
- **the employee and their manager can then discuss and agree what adjustments would improve performance and productivity**
- **the support and cooperation of fellow workers can be enlisted**

2.9

Confidentiality

Guaranteeing confidentiality is one way of encouraging disclosure. In some cases, a breach of confidentiality by an employer may be unlawful.

Remember that:

- **when an employee has told a member of the human resources or occupational health department about the disability in confidence, the employer is deemed under the DDA to know that the person is disabled**
- **if an adjustment is necessary, e.g. time off work, or non standard hours, the employee's line manager will need to know the adjustment is required but neither she nor colleagues need be told the precise medical reasons for it**

Managing adjustments

Many of the adjustments required for people with progressive and fluctuating conditions will be identical to those needed for employees with other types of disability. However, because these conditions are progressive and fluctuating, the issues around employment can be more complex.

Time-keeping

Under the DDA, an employer may need to make a 'reasonable adjustment' by altering a person's working hours. This will very much depend on the condition. Many employees with long-term medical conditions can satisfactorily manage those conditions provided they have a regular work pattern, and are allowed breaks to take medication or a necessary rest. Their needs are predictable and simple adjustments can be made:

- **an employee with a kidney disease requires a special form of dialysis four times a day. Space has been made in the first aid room for dialysis to be undertaken while she is at work**

Some employees will need breaks for regular (psychological) support:

- **an employee who has had an operation for cancer is permitted to telephone his support worker in scheduled breaks and, in emergencies, during working hours**

Some employees will find it difficult to be on time regularly - due, for example, to the effects of medication and difficulties in getting up because of pain and insomnia. In cases of lateness, the line manager should establish with the employee how long the problem is likely to last and what can be done to help get the employee to work on time:

- **as a result of a change in medication, an employee with a mental health problem starts coming in late. Agreement is reached on how she will make up lost time and on a time to review the situation in the future**

Stamina and concentration

Certain levels of stamina are required for particular jobs. With certain progressive or fluctuating conditions, a person's stamina may vary throughout the day or at certain times because of medication or a flare up of pain.

The adjustment called for may be no more than the recognition that the employee's pace of work varies. For example, someone with rheumatoid arthritis may have difficulty in moving round early in the morning, which means they start slowly. Someone with osteoarthritis may get stiffer as the day goes on, which affects their work late in the day.

Flexibility over working hours:

- **an employee with muscular dystrophy must avoid stress. Her employer changes her hours from 9-5 to 10-6 so that she avoids travelling in the rush hour**

- **an employee who takes long-acting medication feels less alert for a while after taking it. His employer allows him to work fewer hours during the week he takes the medication and he makes up the time the following week**

For some people with progressive conditions, it can be difficult to concentrate for long periods of time. This may be exacerbated if their disability is affected by aspects of the office environment, for example, noise:

- **as a result of a brain injury a telephone sales consultant has difficulties in distinguishing between different sounds. Sound absorbing partitions are installed to reduce noise and distractions and the telephone bell has been reprogrammed, so that she can tell when her own phone is ringing**

It may be enough of an adjustment to allow an employee to take more frequent breaks than usual, to have regular snacks, or to arrange a regular change of tasks, to stimulate concentration. It is important to recognise that an individual will usually know best how to deal with these issues.

Memory loss

Some conditions incur memory loss. This may be a side-effect of medication. Being aware of this, the line manager can help to ensure that the individual receives the information needed to do the job, for example, by seeing that he/she has records of meetings whenever possible, or by checking that key information has been received.

There are devices, including functions within computer packages which may be used as a prompt to remind people what their next task is. Careful supervision, using written rather than verbal lists of what can be done, can also be helpful.

Sickness absence management

Many disabled people are rarely sick, and when they are, the reason may be the same as for their non-disabled colleagues – a bad cold or flu.

However, some progressive/fluctuating conditions may present particular problems with regard to absence from work.

Adopting a flexible approach to the management of disability related absence is an important element of good practice towards employees with progressive conditions. What's more, in some cases failure to make reasonable adjustments to sickness absence policies and procedures may amount to unlawful discrimination.

Predictable absences

One of the examples of possible 'reasonable adjustments' listed in the DDA is allowing a disabled employee to be absent during working hours for rehabilitation, assessment or treatment. This will apply to new employees as well as to employees who become disabled, or whose condition becomes worse, during their employment.

For example, an employee with cystic fibrosis needs a few days off each year to attend a specialist centre for a check-up. Her employer gives her special leave. Or an employee's deteriorating arthritis means she needs an operation for a hip replacement.

This form of 'disability leave' is different from sickness absence, whether or not the sickness is directly related to a person's disability. It is more like leave for ante-natal appointments, or maternity leave. It is good practice for employers to introduce a 'disability leave' policy, thus acknowledging the need and right of disabled employees to take special leave to attend medical appointments, hospital check-ups, or to take time off for support or rehabilitation.

Medical appointments (e.g. GPs, consultants, therapists) which may occur during working hours, – often unavoidably – should be allowed where this is reasonable, as paid time off, taking into account frequency and how long the need for the appointments will go on.

- **An employee with Parkinson's disease may need leave to attend physiotherapy sessions one afternoon a week for six weeks, during working hours**

- **An employee with HIV may need time off for counselling and hospital appointments**

With progressive and fluctuating conditions, symptoms can often become worse as a result of stress or tiredness. Managing workloads, and tackling the cause of stress may help reduce the employees need for time off.

The DDA does not require an employer to keep on someone indefinitely if they are constantly absent, but it may require you to keep them longer than a non-disabled employee. You will certainly need to consider flexible options such as working from home or part-time working.

To manage absence it is helpful to differentiate between types of sickness absence:

- **Long term sickness absence – known length**

- **Long term sickness absence – unknown length**

- **Periodic sickness absence – predictable/unpredictable short-term absences**

For more information see Chapter 1.5 – 'Managing sickness absence'.

Retention

It is in your mutual interests that all disabled employees continue to contribute to the organisation as long as possible. Regular review of progress, as part of your normal annual appraisal scheme, is essential:

- **focus on achievements and successes, not on the disability**

- **encourage the individual to assess their own performance. If there have been any changes, establish why**

- **if changes are due to the disability, consider:**
  - **– how existing adjustments might be made more effective**
  - **– whether further adjustments would be helpful or viable, for example part-time working, job sharing or working from home**
  - **– whether medical advice is needed, either from the company medical adviser or the individual's GP**

- **ensure if possible that decisions about future employment reflect mutual agreement**

Annual appraisal

Bristol Age Care engaged Joan Williams as an accounts supervisor, knowing that she had Parkinson's Disease. Computer technology has enabled Joan to fulfil tasks which handwriting problems would have made difficult and her duties have been changed to suit her capabilities. Instead of undertaking site visits involving driving she now does more office-based projects. At her annual appraisal meetings her line manager reviews her progress on the basis of how her talents and skills can continue to be utilised, not on the basis of the limitations her disability increasingly imposes.

2.9 Conclusion

It is extremely important that line managers and supervisors understand that those workplace issues which might normally trigger disciplinary procedures, may in fact be due to disability - and thus need to be managed differently.

If an employee's performance or attendance gives cause for concern, the first step should always be to understand why. If the problem is disability-related there is then a duty to consider reasonable adjustments.

The role of occupational health specialists

Whether considering a new appointment, or dealing with an existing disabled employee, an employer should not automatically refer people with progressive or fluctuating conditions to the occupational health department. This may be discriminatory. However it is good practice to involve this department in establishing good policies and procedures on disability matters.

When you do refer someone to the occupational health department or medical adviser it is important that:

- **they are fully conversant with the employment provisions of the DDA**
- **they understand your policies relating to the employment of disabled people, and their role in determining adjustments**

It may be useful to provide them with disability awareness training.

When medical advisers undertake pre-employment medical examinations, their advice on suitability for employment must relate to the specific requirements of the job, and include recommendations, where appropriate, on any possible adjustments. Medical evidence about a disability cannot justify an adverse employment decision if that disability has no effect on the person's ability to do the work.

If a disabled job applicant insists on confidentiality but does need an adjustment, the medical adviser has a crucial role to play. He has to explain to the organisation what adjustments are needed without divulging the nature of the person's disability.

The role of the medical adviser is also important when he/she knows that an applicant or employee has a progressive condition but the symptoms are not yet apparent. The medical adviser should advise the individual of (a) their rights under the DDA and (b) the pros and cons of disclosure, and continue to monitor developments.

The relationship between the employer, the employee with a progressive or fluctuating condition and the medical adviser should be such that decisions on future employment are reached on the basis of mutual agreement.

Occupational pension and insurance schemes

It is unlawful to bar someone from joining an occupational pension scheme just because they have a disability. It is however permissible to exclude someone from the scheme if the costs of providing benefits would be substantially greater than for a non-disabled employee. The employer would need actuarial advice and/or medical evidence to justify such exclusion.

The duty of reasonable adjustment does not apply to the provision of benefits under an occupational pension scheme. However, while the law may allow you to treat disabled people differently to others, as a matter of good practice you should consider:

- **whether the scheme can be adapted to provide all employees, including those with progressive/fluctuating conditions, with the same benefits, or**
- **what alternative provision might be made for people with such conditions**

In general, the larger the employer the more likely it is that all entrants to the organisation are admitted to the pension scheme. The DDA makes broadly similar provisions for group insurance schemes as for occupational schemes. So you should also consider what you can do to ensure that people with progressive/fluctuating conditions enjoy the same insurance benefits as others. If your present insurer bars people with particular disabilities it may be worth trying other insurance companies. If you cannot find alternative cover, you might offer other benefits of a similar value.

2.9

Policy and training

The most important single adjustment you need to make may well be in attitude. Crucial to this are policies and training.

It is essential that:

- **everyone in your organisation is aware that your equal opportunity and disability policies cover people with progressive and fluctuating conditions**
- **information about these conditions is included in: (a) training on managing disability given to line managers and human resource specialists (b) disability awareness training for employees**

Making your policies work

Fellow workers may regard adjustments as privileged treatment - particularly adjustments to working hours. It is important therefore, that everyone knows what your policy is and why, in general, adjustments are made. They should understand that it is fair play to treat someone differently, and that each person and each situation is unique. If objections are raised they should be fully discussed (unless an employee has asked that confidentiality is observed). Any harassment should be firmly dealt with.

2.9

In the long run, experience shows that sound retention policies lead to all employees feeling more secure in the knowledge that their employer will treat them fairly should they become disabled themselves.

Help, advice and information can be obtained from the following organisations

(Contact details are provided at the back of this book).

- **AbilityNet**
- **Disability Rights Commission**
- **Employers' Forum on Disability**
- **Jobcentre Plus**
- **The Long-Term Medical Conditions Alliance**
- **The Society of Occupational Medicine**

A PRACTICAL GUIDE TO

employment adjustments for people with mental health problems

- Tackling the causes of mental health problems
- Working with people with mental health problems
- Disclosure and confidentiality
- Recruitment and selection
- Adjustments in employment
- The role of the supervisor

2.10

The DDA

Under the Disability Discrimination Act (DDA) (1995) it is unlawful for an employer to treat a disabled applicant for a job, or an employee, less favourably, without justification. An employer also has a duty under the DDA to make reasonable adjustments to prevent a disabled employee from being placed at a substantial disadvantage by any physical feature of the premises, or by working arrangements. The duty applies to all aspects of employment, including recruitment and selection, training, transfer, career development and retention.

The DDA defines a disabled person as someone who has, or had, "a physical or mental impairment, which has a substantial and long-term adverse effect" on their ability to carry out normal day-to-day activities. "Long-term" means that it must have lasted, or be expected to last, at least 12 months.

Normal day-to-day activities include memory or ability to concentrate, learn or understand. A mental health problem is covered by the DDA providing that it is "recognised by a respected body of medical opinion". Thus, mental health problems ranging from manic depressive conditions could be within the scope of the DDA.

'Long-term' means that the disability must have lasted, or be expected to last, at least 12 months. People disabled due to recurring or episodic conditions are covered if the substantial adverse effects are likely to recur beyond twelve months after the first occurrence. For example, someone with manic depression who has an episode lasting a few weeks, and then a lengthy period of remission, could be covered.

Someone with a mental health problem whose symptoms are controlled by medication may also be covered.

A person who once had a disability which is covered by the DDA, but has recovered from the disability, is protected. For example, it would be unlawful to discriminate against a job applicant or employee who experienced a nervous breakdown five years ago.

Tackling the causes

2.10 Mental health problems are one of the major causes of certified sickness absence and account annually for the loss of over 90 million working days (Department of Health). This is clearly damaging to productivity, interpersonal relationships, staff turnover and individual performance. Effective management, which includes making adjustments for people with mental health problems and implementation of strategy that promotes a healthy working environment, will be a significant step towards managing and minimising sickness absence.

Working with people with mental health problems

Despite gradually changing attitudes, there continues to be considerable discrimination against people with mental health problems, even though three in ten employees will have a mental health problem in any year (Office for National Statistics).

People with mental health problems are not a homogeneous group. Many need no adjustments at all, particularly if they are given an element of genuine control over how and when they do their job. The most important single adjustment you need to make may well be in the realm of attitudes and assumptions. It is essential that:

- **everyone in your organisation is aware that your equal opportunity and disability policies cover people with mental health problems**
- **information about mental health problems is included in:**

  a **training on managing disability given to line managers and HR specialists**

  b **disability awareness training**

Though the DDA and the Code of Practice make a number of specific provisions for people with mental health problems, ambiguities do exist, for example, in connection with stress and stress-related conditions. Adopting best practice is likely to be far more helpful than a mere compliance approach. Therefore, if you are uncertain whether an individual is covered by the Act, it would be prudent to assume that they are covered, and to consider what adjustments, if any, are necessary for them to do the job.

There are no pre-determined solutions. An adjustment that suits one person may not suit another person with apparently the same diagnosis or problem. The individual is often the most informed, so ask the employee if they need any adjustments.

Changing attitudes

Attitudes and views on mental health problems have been radically altered at Royal Sun Alliance, Ipswich, as a result of providing work placements for members of a local Clubhouse (see the Help and information section at the back of this book). The placements are for people with severe or enduring mental health problems who would like to return to regular employment. Over the past three years the company's Ipswich offices have regularly employed Clubhouse members in routine posts lasting on average six months, in a wide range of departments. This has demonstrated to both management and staff how well people with various mental impairments can perform, and done much to change misconceptions and misunderstandings about health problems.

Disclosure

Because of stigma and fear of discrimination, job applicants and employees are often unwilling to reveal that they have, or have had, a mental health problem. Indeed, they may not think of themselves as 'disabled', and may not require adjustments.
An individual who has, or has had, a mental health problem may choose not to disclose the problem when they are first appointed, or indeed until they have been in a job for some time.
If it is known that there is a willingness to make reasonable adjustments for all disabled applicants and employees, people with mental health problems will be much more likely to trust the employer and colleagues and be open. Acceptance is morale boosting; fear of being 'found out' can be stressful and sap confidence.

Disclosure makes it possible for:

- **employees and managers to agree what adjustments would improve performance and productivity**
- **support of fellow-workers to be enlisted**

All employees should understand the concept of adjustment and its place in your equal opportunity policy. This helps to ensure that when a colleague benefits from an adjustment, other employees accept it, recognising that it is part of your management culture, and that ultimately everyone will benefit.

Confidentiality

If you encourage employees to declare any mental health problems, they should also know you will respect requests for confidentiality.
Remember that:

- when an employee has told the human resources or occupational health department about their disability in confidence, the employer is deemed under the DDA to know that the person is disabled, and therefore under a duty to consider reasonable adjustments

- if an adjustment is necessary, e.g. time off work or a partitioned workspace, the employee's supervisor will need to know that the adjustment is required. However, neither supervisor nor fellow workers need to be told the precise medical reasons for it, just the nature of the adjustment

2.10

Job descriptions

When drawing up job descriptions and candidate specifications:

- distinguish between essential and desirable requirements. You can then be flexible when considering adjustments such as re-allocating work

- concentrate on what is to be achieved in the job rather than how it is to be achieved. Someone with a mental health problem may simply do things differently

- ensure that the mental or emotional requirements of the job have been identified, but avoid generalities such as 'the ability to work under pressure or in stressful situations'

- focus on what is actually required, for example, 'the ability to work with competing priorities', 'the need to meet deadlines', or 'the ability to deal with all members of the public

Recruitment and selection

Someone with a mental health problem may not have filled in an application form for some time and therefore welcome guidelines or assistance. It might also help them to know what to expect at interview.

Remember that an applicant may:

- wish to be accompanied by a friend or adviser

- apply for a job for which they are over-qualified because they need to regain confidence after recovering from a mental health problem

- have gaps in their c.v. due to a mental health problem

- have done voluntary work, for which they can give a referee

- have had difficulties in previous employment, because adjustments were not made

- appear to have poor interpersonal skills

If the selection process involves tests, the candidate may need:

- **extra time**

- **to take a written test orally**

- **an individual rather than a group process**

If the candidate has disclosed a current or previous mental health problem:

- **focus on the candidate's ability to do the job and give them as much opportunity as possible to demonstrate their suitability**

- **do not make assumptions!**

It may be helpful to see the interview as a two-stage process. The first stage is a discussion about issues such as the job requirements, experience of the employee etc. The second stage should include a discussion on what adjustments, if any, are needed.

Adjustments at work

During induction and initial training, an employee who has, or has had, a mental health problem, may need a particularly clear and thorough explanation of what is required of them. During the first few months of employment, adjustments may be necessary in the form of extra support, feedback and reassurance.

If an employee's attendance, performance or behaviour gives cause for concern the first step should always be to find out why. If the problem is disability-related, an adjustment can then be considered. You should discuss any adjustment with the individual.

a Absence from work:

The underlying cause of frequent short sickness absences and long term sickness absence is often due to a mental health problem - which may not be apparent from the declared or medically certificated cause of absence. In the case of long-term absence it is important to keep in touch with the individual, and attempt to determine if reasonable adjustments are required An absence due to a mental health problem might fall within the meaning of a disability under the DDA.

Adjustments might include:

- **flexibility in how your sick pay policies are applied, e.g. exceeding normal entitlement**

- **flexibility in the rules applying to annual holidays. For example, you might allow someone to use unscheduled annual holiday entitlement at short notice**

It is useful to see Chapter 1.5 – 'Managing sickness absence'.

Rehabilitation after long term absence

HSBC operates a rehabilitation policy for employees who have undergone a long-term absence from work due to a variety of health issues, including

2.10

stress and depression. There is a consultation process involving the individual, their line manager, the occupational health manager, the human resource department and the individual's GP and consultant. This ensures that both the individual and line manager are advised correctly in respect of the individual's capacity and potential for resuming their role. The process also determines any adjustments that could be made to accommodate the employee. If appropriate, there is a phased return to work, usually over a period of weeks, during which the individual gradually increases the hours/days worked until, if successful, they are able to resume their normal work pattern.

b Working arrangements:

Adjustments might include:

- **re-arranging responsibilities/tasks, for example, exchanging a single demanding project for a job consisting of a number of smaller tasks**
- **flexible working hours, including part-time working, job-sharing or working from home for some or all of the time**
- **permission to talk to a support professional by phone during the working day**
- **transferring the employee to another job**

c Concentration/memory:

Occasionally people with mental health problems experience difficulties with concentration and/or memory. Adjustments might include:

- **providing room dividers, partitions or other soundproofing or visual barriers**
- **occasional or permanent home-working**
- **reducing noise in the work environment**

Written instructions may help decrease anxiety, increase confidence, provide a structure for work for people who have some difficulty in organising themselves, or who have concentration difficulties.

Short-term memory loss or lapses in memory may likewise be overcome with the help of written instructions. For someone who has problems remembering dates, appointments and phone numbers an electronic organiser with an alarm may be the answer.

d Side effects of medication:

Some medication may cause grogginess in the mornings, or make waking difficult, resulting in the employee being late. Flexible working hours may be a viable option.

If medication causes thirst and a constant need for fluids, the employee may need ready access to drinks.

Occasionally medication for certain mental health problems may cause minor tremor, which affects fine motor control, triggering the need for adjustments.

There may be no side effects at all from medication.

e Medical appointments:

If an employee has to attend medical appointments (e.g. GP, consultant, or therapist) during working hours, it would be best practice to allow paid time off.

If, however, the appointments go on for a long time, and/or the financial viability of the organisation is affected, you might need to consider other arrangements, for example time off or a time-in-lieu arrangement. An employee attending weekly therapy sessions might be allowed to take a longer lunch break and the time made up later.

f Unusual behaviour:

People with a mental health problem may on occasions behave in ways others regard as 'strange' (e.g. humming or talking to themselves) yet do their job satisfactorily. A reasonable adjustment could be simply to secure fellow workers' tolerance and understanding.

g Technology:

E-mail may be the solution for someone who finds face to face communication difficult.

If telephone calls exacerbate anxiety, voice-mail can be used to take messages with no loss of overall response time.

Medical advice

There will be situations where you feel a need for medical advice. You may, for example, have concerns about an applicant's ability to do the job on health grounds, or you may be concerned that a particular aspect of the job might cause the recurrence of a previous medical health problem.

Or you may be concerned when:

- **an employee is frequently off sick for short periods or has a lengthy spell of sickness absence**
- **an employee is returning to work after a period of rehabilitation**
- **an employee is being considered for promotion**

Before seeking medical advice you should:

- **talk to the applicant or employee**
- **establish who is the most appropriate professional to consult**

- **obtain the employee's permission before contacting a GP, occupational health or other mental health specialist**

In seeking medical advice you should ask only specific, job or employment-related questions, for example making it clear that you want to consider reasonable adjustments.

You are responsible for assessing the quality and relevance of medical advice. You should not take decisions about any aspect of an individual's employment on the basis of medical advice without considering the specific work context.

2.10

Stress

It is a common misconception that people who have had a mental health problem cannot tolerate stress. In fact we all need a certain amount of stress to remain healthy and alert, and we can all be damaged by too much. People with mental health problems have demonstrated their ability to do challenging work under testing conditions. Nevertheless, stress and stress-related problems make up a significant proportion of the certified sickness absence statistics. If stress goes unrelieved it can lead to a wide range of mental health problems, including breakdown, which could fall within the definition of a disability. Causes of stress at work include:

- **lack of control over work. Employees often work better if they have more freedom in planning their work, making their own decisions and dealing with problems on their own**
- **lack of recognition and positive feedback**
- **under-use of skills**
- **too much or not enough work**
- **work that is repetitive or monotonous, or that is over-familiar and presents no new challenges**
- **uncertainty about what is expected or required in the job, about the job itself and about the future of the organisation**

Carrying out an audit of your business may alert you to causes of stress. You could ask staff about:

- **what they value about the organisation**
- **what helps them within their role and within the organisation**
- **what changes they would like to happen**
- **what they find frustrating about their role and within the organisation**

You will need to consider confidentiality and ensure that the exercise is seen as credible. The exercise should be repeated to monitor the success of any strategies that result and to continually aid in developing your organisation.

The role of the supervisor

The role of the immediate supervisor is crucial in the management of any adjustment, but it is especially important in the case of employees with mental health problems. You should:

- **select supervisors for their interpersonal skills as well as for technical ability**
- **train them in the causes and manifestations of stress and mental health problems at work and in what might be reasonable adjustments**
- **recognise that dealing with mental health problems can be time-consuming and demanding, and**
- **give due weight to their supervisor's success in managing adjustments and related issues, e.g. in their annual appraisal**

Supervisors should:

- **know how much authority they have to agree adjustments**
- **adopt a consultative approach, working with the individual and the team to solve problems jointly**
- **know how to manage fellow workers should they perceive an adjustment to be preferential treatment**
- **know where to go for advice, information and support**

Co-worker support

Janey Antoniou worked as a scientific officer with the Medical Research Council for over 12 years. The organisation is goal-oriented, the pace of work is fast and there is an open style of management. The support and understanding of co-workers was probably the main adjustment enabling Janey to remain in employment and work to exacting standards. Her line manager's understanding of schizophrenia and his ability to forestall problems was also extremely important. He had Janey's permission to contact her key worker if she showed signs of difficulties. Another factor was the flexibility over hours which her work allowed. Janey never exceeded her entitlement to paid sick leave.

Help, advice and information can be obtained from the following organisations

(Contact details are provided at the back of this book).

- **Employers' Forum on Disability**
- **Jobcentre Plus**
- **The Manic Depression Fellowship**
- **Mind**
- **National Clubhouse Association**
- **Scottish Association for Mental Health**
- **Shaw Trust Information Resource (STIR)**

A PRACTICAL GUIDE TO

employment adjustments for dyslexic people

- Dyslexia, the facts
- Recruitment and promotion
- Adjustments in employment
- Help, advice and information

2.11

Introduction

Under the Disability Discrimination Act (DDA) it is unlawful for an employer to treat a disabled applicant or employee less favourably because of their disability without justification.

The employer has a duty to make 'reasonable adjustments' if a disabled person or employee is at a substantial disadvantage in relation to a non-disabled person. The duty of adjustments applies to physical features of an employers' premises (e.g. buildings, fittings and equipment), and employment factors, including recruitment and selection, promotion, training, transfer, career development and retention.

It makes good business sense to make adjustments. Dyslexic people represent a significant resource in the labour market and at work their talents are often under utilised. Dyslexic people may require adjustments in the workplace - which can be simple and inexpensive. Without such adjustments, good candidates may not apply and excellent employees may be lost.

This section provides practical guidance on the type of adjustments that can be considered. It can also be given to employees to help them identify their needs and adopt solutions for a better working environment, in discussion with their employer.

Dyslexia, the facts

It is suggested that up to 10% of the population show some signs of dyslexia. It occurs independent of ability; intellectual and creative ability is not impaired. Dyslexia is a difficulty in processing information and is linked to short-term memory and visual co-ordination. The areas primarily affected are reading, writing, spelling, numeracy, time-keeping and personal organisation. These difficulties can have a secondary effect on an individual's self-confidence and lead to anxiety, frustration and low self-esteem.

An individual may not realise they have dyslexia. Job or organisational change could bring this to light, for example, someone who has access to secretarial support which is then withdrawn.

2.11

A dyslexic person will often have particular talents as well as difficulties, for example the person may be a fast thinker, a good problem solver, and have excellent visual and spatial awareness. Making adjustments and releasing the potential of dyslexic employees can have a positive effect on an organisation as it unlocks different ways of tackling problems and making decisions.

Royal Mail Engineering

Martin Freston, is dyslexic, and was formerly employed by Royal Mail Engineering as the Director and General Manager. He believes the way dyslexia was treated in the British Educational system in the 1950s and 1960s, has impeded his ability to gain the qualifications to attend university. Therefore, Martin has adopted new skills. He approaches problems, handles communication and finds solutions in a different way because his abilities do not include high-level reading or writing skills. Martin comments: "I think it's about delivering a product or service, or whatever you're doing, to the customers and if you can do that by whatever route you adopt, then that is the measure of success."

Recruitment and promotion

When drawing up job descriptions and candidate specifications, ensure that you do not needlessly exclude a dyslexic person:

- **be flexible. Very often minor changes can make a significant difference**
- **concentrate on what is to be achieved in a job rather than how it is to be achieved. A dyslexic person may simply do things differently**

Application forms:

- **use a simple, clear type face**
- **send the application form by email or disc so that the individual need not be concerned about written presentation and can also use a spell checker**
- **where possible, use matt, pastel coloured paper. Some forms of dyslexia are exacerbated by colour, with black against white often the worst. Pastel colours will reduce the glare**

Aptitude and other tests

- **consult dyslexic applicants in advance so that necessary adjustments can be made**
- **ensure that test instructions are clearly read aloud**
- **allow more time for dyslexic candidates**
- **if adjustments are unsuitable be prepared to waive the test. There are often equally satisfactory ways of getting the information**

Adjustments in employment

Some people may be unaware that they are dyslexic. If you believe that either yourself or one of your employees is dyslexic, the British Dyslexia Association has produced a "diagnostic" tick list which can be used prior to professional assessment. A professional assessment may be required to identify specific needs, but many people with dyslexia require little in the way of support beyond the acceptance that they will need to approach tasks differently.

If an assessment is required, it is important to brief the specialist on the employee's occupation. Receiving a report that only records the nature of the employee's dyslexia will not be useful. Explain to the specialist that you need to know how this will affect the individual at work and what sort of adjustments may help the employee perform more effectively at work. The specialist should be made aware that disability is a discrimination issue and that there is a duty to make reasonable adjustments to working practices and the working environment under the DDA.

Most dyslexic people, once they understand their disability, are inventive in developing coping strategies that enable them not only to learn and work effectively, but also to often adopt a fresh approach to problem solving.

As the severity of dyslexia varies, so do the strategies that help dyslexic people overcome problems in employment. The majority of adjustments are inexpensive and uncomplicated. However, should additional costs be incurred (e.g. a voice activated computer or reader), the employer can apply for funding through the Government's Access to Work Scheme.

The strategies in this briefing paper are suggestions that have proved successful for many. A particular employee may require none, one or several of the strategies suggested, which have been categorised as follows:

1. **Written Communication**
2. **Verbal Communication**
3. **Time and Work Planning**
4. **General**

Within each category are a number of suggestions. The person's pattern of dyslexia may make some of these inappropriate. For example, if a person has difficulty in reading, then asking them to take notes and check them as a way of remembering and following verbal instructions will not be appropriate. Instead, encouraging the employee to use a tape recorder may be the best solution. Try out some of the adjustments until the person finds the best way of working. Remember, do not assume that as the employer, you know best – **always** consult the individual.

2.11

1. Written Communication

General difficulty with reading:

- **give verbal rather than written instructions**
- **highlight salient points in documents**
- **use voice mail as opposed to written memos**
- **use speech to text software**
- **supply/use a reading machine – or allocate someone else to read aloud**
- **provide information on coloured paper (find out which colour helps the person to read the best) and coloured notepads to write on**
- **set up the computer screen with a coloured background to documents**

Difficulty with reading and writing:

- **allow plenty of time to read and complete the task (e.g. allow the individual to take documents home to read)**
- **examine other ways of giving the same information to avoid reading**
- **discuss the material with the employee; give summaries and/or key points**
- **utilise information given through alternative media sources, (e.g. audio or video tape) or use drawings, diagrams and flow charts**
- **allocate someone else to write by hand for them**
- **use tape recorders**
- **use speech to text software**

Spelling and grammar errors:

- **proof read work**
- **install spell checking programmes on all computers**

Comax

Louise Herd was employed as a receptionist by Comax (formerly part of DERA). Dyslexia affects her reading, writing and spelling abilities. Initially Louise was very nervous, possessed little self-confidence and was reluctant to admit her difficulties. She eventually approached her line manager and between them they devised a form which is now used by anyone at reception, in order to successfully help take messages and visitors' details. Her work colleagues are supportive and she now has no qualms to say that she is dyslexic or to ask guests to spell out their details. Her managers say that she has grown visibly in confidence and is an effective team member. Louise says: "If your colleagues believe in you, then your confidence can only grow."

2. Verbal Communication

Difficulty remembering and following verbal instructions:

- **give instructions one at a time**
- **communicate instructions slowly and clearly in a quiet location**
- **write down important information**
- **demonstrate and supervise tasks or projects**
- **encourage the person to take notes and then check them**
- **ask instructions to be repeated back, to confirm that the information has been understood correctly**
- **write a memo outlining a plan of action**
- **use a tape recorder or Dictaphone to record important instructions**
- **back-up multiple instructions in writing or with diagrams**

Difficulty with hidden meanings in conversation:

- **give clear, concise and direct instructions; do not hint, or make assumptions that you have been understood**

3. Time and Work Planning

Concentration difficulties/distractions:

- **make sure the workspace is quiet and away from distractions (e.g. away from doors, busy phones, loud machinery)**
- **allocate a private workspace if possible**
- **where feasible, allow an employee to work from home occasionally**
- **provide a quiet working environment for a dyslexic employee by allocating libraries, file rooms, private offices, store rooms and other enclosed areas when others are not using them**

Coping with interruptions:

- **use a "DO NOT DISTURB" sign when specific tasks require intense concentration**

2.11

- **encourage other co-workers not to disturb the person unless absolutely necessary**
- **when interrupting, allow the person to pause and write down what they are doing to refer to when resuming work**
- **ensure that each task is completed before starting another**
- **encourage outgoing rather than incoming calls. Offer training in how to use the telephone effectively, (e.g. jotting down key points before making the call)**
- **organise quiet working times for certain hours of the day, and encourage interruptions specifically during this time**

Remembering appointments, deadlines etc.:

- **remind the person of important deadlines and review priorities regularly**
- **hang a wall planner that visually highlights daily/monthly appointments, deadlines, tasks, projects etc.**
- **supply an alarm watch**
- **encourage the employee to use the daily calendar and alarm features on his/her computer**

Organisation of property:

- **ensure that work areas are organised, neat and tidy**
- **keep items where they can be clearly seen, (e.g. shelves or bulletin boards)**
- **ensure the team returns important items in the same place each time**
- **colour code items**
- **ensure work areas are well lit**

Organising workflows:

- **supply and use a wall planner**
- **prioritise important tasks**
- **create a daily, dated "TO DO" list**
- **use diaries**
- **write a layout for regular tasks with appropriate prompts (e.g. for meetings or taking notes)**
- **allow extra time for unforeseen occurrences**
- **decide how long a task should take and use a timer to keep to deadlines**
- **build planning time into each day**

4. General Difficulties

Reversing numbers:

- **encourage the person to say the numbers out loud, write them down, or press the calculator keys, check that the figures have been understood**

- **supply a talking calculator**

Directional difficulties:

- **always try to use the same route**

- **show the route and note visual landmarks**

- **give time to practice going from one place to another**

- **supply detailed maps**

Short term memory especially names, numbers and lists:

- **use mnemonic devices and acronyms**

- **organise details on paper so that they can be referred to easily, using diagrams or flow charts**

- **check back understanding**

- **use multi-sensory learning techniques (e.g. read material onto a tape machine and then play it back whilst re-reading)**

- **use computer software; sometimes well developed programme menus and help features are useful**

- **use a calculator**

QinetiQ

A manager employed by QinetiQ (formerly part of DERA) had always succeeded without his employers being aware that he was dyslexic, until he was given the added responsibility of writing staff appraisal reports. He approached his line manager, who in conjunction with training and personnel arranged an assessment for dyslexia. The assessor recommended that the manager have a weekly one-to-one session with a dyslexia specialist to help him devise coping strategies in the work place. Following these sessions, the individual is now confident and effective in his report writing. QinetiQ bore the cost for this and as personnel manager, Tina Harris states, "We at QinetiQ recognise that investing in this manager's training and giving support to his development, has benefited both the individual and the organisation."

The Employers' Forum on Disability gratefully acknowledges the help that it has received in preparing this section from the Adult Dyslexia & Skills Development Centre, the British Dyslexia Association.

Help, advice and information can be obtained from the following organisations

(Contact details are provided at the back of this book).

- **Adult Dyslexia Organisation**
- **Adult Dyslexia and Skills**
- **British Dyslexia Association**
- **Development Centre**
- **Dyslexia Institute**
- **Employers Forum on Disability**
- **Jobcentre Plus**
- **Saville and Holdsworth**

2.11

A PRACTICAL GUIDE TO

employment adjustments for people with upper limb disorders and repetitive strain injuries

2.12

This section provides an overview of the type of adjustments that can be considered for people who have upper limb disorders (ULDs), including those referred to as repetitive strain injuries (RSI). It also offers general advice on practical approaches to such adjustments.

The section recognises that some of these conditions are work-related. It therefore attempts to bridge the gap between the adjustments required under the Disability Discrimination Act and the risk assessments and ergonomic considerations required under health and safety legislation, so as to develop integrated management approaches. This is not a complicated process but it is important to note that the terminology in this section will differ depending on which particular piece of legislation is under discussion.

This section will be useful for personnel, human resources, occupational health, recruitment and training specialists and line managers. It can also be given to employees and their representatives, to help them identify their needs and adopt solutions for a better working environment, in consultation with their employer. It is not intended as a substitute for specialist advice or assessment in specific cases, and does not cover medical treatment. Sources of further information, specialist advice and assistance are listed for reference at the end of this book.

Introduction

Under the Disability Discrimination Act it is unlawful for an employer to treat a disabled applicant or an employee less favourably for a reason related to their disability, without justification.

2.12

The DDA defines a disabled person as someone who has "a physical or mental impairment which has a substantial and long-term adverse effect" on a person's ability to carry out normal day-to-day activities. "Long-term" means that it must have lasted, or be expected to last, at least 12 months. Progressive or fluctuating conditions can also qualify where there are likely to be future or recurrent substantial adverse effects. People with disabilities due to upper limb disorders and repetitive strain injury may not consider themselves disabled but the DDA definition of disability may well apply.

Our advice is to take a positive attitude towards resolving problems rather than spending time and money trying to establish if someone is covered by the Act.

Upper limb disorders and RSI – an overview

"Upper limb disorders" (ULDs) is an umbrella term which covers people with a wide variety of musculo-skeletal conditions and related disabilities, including those commonly referred to as Repetitive Strain Injury (RSI) and Cumulative Trauma Disorder (CTD). These conditions are also sometimes referred to as "work-related upper limb disorders" (WRULDs).

They predominantly involve disorders of the tendons, nerves and/or muscles. They are associated with:

- **repetitive actions and forceful exertion (especially in combination)**
- **awkward movements**
- **vibration**
- **localised mechanical stress**
- **poor work organisation and occupational stress**
- **cold**

Many factors and risks can combine to cause upper limb disorders and repetitive strain injuries, including job design, equipment, the work environment, the duration and intensity of work activities and stress.

Diagnosis

Upper limb disorders are not always recognised or correctly diagnosed. There is disagreement and confusion around terminology and definitions as well as causes. Generally, localised conditions (e.g. "tennis elbow") are easier to diagnose – and better understood medically – than the less localised or "diffuse" conditions which are more common but without clear diagnosis. There can be overlap, and some symptoms are also similar to muscle fatigue. Expert diagnosis is important – there are a variety of conditions involving different types of injury or disability. They may require different types of treatment, adjustments and management approaches.

Legal arguments are rife in this area. But in an Employment Tribunal case taken under the DDA, Palmer v Caradon Mira Ltd, (1400115/98), the tribunal found in favour of the applicant and RSI was recognised as a disability.

Case law –
Palmer V Caradon Mira Ltd

Ms Palmer worked for Caradon Mira as a machine operator from October 1989 until her dismissal in December 1997. In January 1996 she was placed into a new job requiring repetitive work and developed pain in her right hand and forearm. She complained and was relocated after reasonable adjustments proved ineffective. She then took sick leave. The company had a policy for job rotation of staff with upper limb disorders. This policy proved ineffective. Despite task rotation her pain continued. The employers recognised that the work exacerbated her condition, but claimed that no alternative was available. Further sick leave in July resulted in a medical assessment which stated that Ms. Palmer had a upper limb disorders and the situation would need to be reviewed in a month. The review was never conducted. Instead, Ms. Palmer was dismissed in December. The tribunal held that: the employers had not reasonably informed themselves of the applicant's condition; had not adequately investigated alternative employment; had not conducted a proper medical enquiry and had not made sufficient reasonable adjustments, for example an adjustable bench and time off for physiotherapy.

Examples of upper limb disorders include the following specific medical conditions:

- **Tenosynovitis**
- **Tendinitis**
- **Lateral epicondylitis ("tennis elbow")**
- **Medical epicondylitis ("golfer's elbow")**
- **De Quervain's disease**
- **Trigger finger**
- **Bursitis**
- **Beat conditions**
- **Rotator cuff syndrome**
- **Carpal tunnel syndrome**
- **Cubital tunnel syndrome**
- **Reflex sympathetic dystrophy**
- **Writer's cramp**
- **Mylagia**
- **Frozen shoulder**
- **Vibration-induced white finger**

These conditions can also affect people's personal lives and their ability to travel to and from work, even by public transport. Normal everyday tasks at home as well as at work, and sleep patterns, can be affected.

Symptoms

Symptoms of upper limb disorders and repetitive strain injuries can include muscular fatigue, pain, cramp, swelling, numbness, difficulty in movement and general discomfort. These can persist or

2.12

become worse after work, not just when performing specific tasks. They can affect the neck, shoulders, arms, elbows, wrists, hands and fingers, with related pain elsewhere in the body.

Different people will be affected in different ways. Onset can be gradual, often with minor symptoms in the early stages. But these conditions are generally progressive and cumulative. They can also develop rapidly, especially where workloads, pacing of work or other demands are suddenly increased or intensified. Individual experiences may vary but all, or any, of these symptoms should be regarded as significant. Long-term disabilities can result if they are ignored.

Symptoms can be associated with jobs requiring repetitive finger, hand or arm movements, or movement involving twisting, squeezing, hammering, pounding, pushing, pulling, lifting or reaching. Static or fixed posture can also be a problem. Muscles, nerves and ligaments that are not moved or stretched during the working day can also tighten through lack of use. This in turn affects circulation which can lead to inflammation and pain, caused by sensory damage to the nerves.

Who is affected

Upper limb disorders affect many people. For example:

The Trade Union Congress estimate that over 200,000 people a year take time off due to RSI and that another 200,000 suffer in silence. The cost is estimated to be over £3 billion from sickness payments, lost production and retraining.

Recent research published by the Health and Safety Executive (HSE) looking at problems faced by checkout operators in UK supermarkets, most of whom work part-time, showed that over half of all cashiers will report either back pain or neck/arm pain or both. In a substantial number of cases, the problems will result in sickness absence.

What jobs are affected

Upper limb disorders are widespread. They can affect people in different sectors and different jobs - office-based and manual - and are not, as is so often assumed, confined to computer operators. Examples include:

- **repetitive assembly work**
- **inspection and packing**
- **poultry and food processing**
- **laboratory technicians**
- **cleaning and catering**
- **armed forces**
- **cashiers / check-out operators**
- **textile and garments workers**
- **electronics and telecoms workers**
- **display screen equipment users**
- **carpentry and construction work**

Changes in work, working conditions and technology mean that the incidence of upper limb disorders is increasing in certain areas, particularly information technology and processing.

Driving and upper limb disorders

In 1996, in Edmonton, Canada, the largest incidence of ULD-related complaints came from public transit. The problems were occurring amongst those who were driving buses all the time. Most buses did not have power steering; drivers wrestling with steering wheels complained of arm and wrist pain. It was therefore decided that when buses came in for scheduled maintenance, they would be fitted with power steering and a new seat. The refitting procedure was slow and as an interim adjustment, the company regularly rotated the drivers between the older buses and the newer versions, thus lessening the effects and incidence of upper limb disorder related conditions, sickness absence rates and low morale within the workforce.

The legislative framework: the DDA

Employers have a duty under the DDA to make a "reasonable adjustment" if a disabled applicant or employee is at a substantial disadvantage in relation to others. The duty of adjustment applies to the physical features of an employer's premises, the way the work is organised and carried out, the working conditions and environment, and employment factors, including recruitment, promotion, training, transfer, career development and retention. Employers will have discriminated if in those circumstances they fail to provide reasonable adjustments and cannot justify that failure, or if they treat disabled employees less favorably in relation to their health and safety. The DDA places a duty on employers to make such adjustments whenever it is reasonable to do so. General guidance on what is reasonable is provided within the Act itself and in the accompanying Code of Practice.

Making adjustments to employment arrangements

You will need to consider making reasonable adjustments: when a disabled person with an upper limb disorder or RSI applies to you for a job; when an existing employee develops a disabling condition of this kind, when the effects of the disability change or increase; when there is a change in the disabled person's workplace, equipment or activities; or when a disabled person requires any form of training.

The DDA makes it unlawful for an employer to treat a disabled person less favorably, for a reason relating to their disability, without justification. Less favourable treatment can be legally justified where there is a material and substantial reason. Health and safety concerns may constitute such a reason but it is important, firstly, to consider whether reasonable adjustments can resolve the problem.

The legislative framework: Health and Safety at Work

Under the Health and Safety at Work Act 1974 (HSWA), employers have a duty to provide, amongst other things,

2.12

a safe system of work and to "ensure, as far as is reasonably practicable, the health, safety and welfare at work of all employees".

The Management of Health and Safety at Work Regulations 1992 (the "Management Regulations") outline legal duties to assess risks to health and safety of employees and others arising from the work or workplace involved. The Health and Safety at Work Regulations apply to all organisations regardless of size (see Chapter 1.4 – 'A practical guide to Health and Safety and the DDA').

Employers must use a competent person to assist them in assessing risks and implementing protective measures (competence involves having the necessary relevant skills, knowledge and experience to undertake the task). Employers must also:

- **make a "suitable and sufficient" assessment of risks to the person(s) concerned "in good time"**

- **consult and co-operate with others, including contractors and safety representatives**

- **so far as is reasonably practicable remove or reduce any risks to people, including risks to disabled staff and others already in employment**

- **monitor, review and if necessary revise preventive measures to ensure they are effective**

- **provide information, instruction, training and supervision for staff**

Where five or more people are employed, employers are required to record significant findings of risk assessments in writing and identify any groups of workers particularly at risk. The Approved Code of Practice (ACoP) accompanying the Management Regulations refers to disabled staff as one such group. Some people with upper limb disorders or repetitive strain injury may be included here.

These general duties to assess and control risks to all staff, including those with upper limb disorders, are also reflected in specific regulations such as:

- **the Display Screen Equipment Regulations 1992**

- **the Manual Handling Regulations 1992**

- **the Provision and use of Work Equipment Regulations 1998**

The Manual Handling Regulations 1992 require employers to avoid manual handling wherever practical. When avoidance is not practical, the employer has to assess risks to health, including taking into account the capabilities of the person lifting, and take steps to reduce the risks. Additional requirements affecting workplaces and that are also relevant for people with upper limb disorders and RSI include The Workplace (Health Safety and Welfare) Regulations 1992 and The

Working Time Regulations 1998. These recognise, amongst other things, the need to limit or adjust patterns of work and rest to prevent risks to employee health and safety.

Assessment – general principles

Workplace assessments should be built into a rehabilitation programme. The assessments can aid recovery and/or return to work, and prevent recurrence or further disability. Individuals with upper limb disorders and RSI will naturally vary in age, size, shape and gender, in the way they carry out their jobs, and in the nature and extent of their disability and how it affects them and their work. Assessments must take individual differences and preferences into account, as well as work duties.

Your company may already have an appointed person who carries out risk assessments. If not, The Society of Occupational Medicine has a list of Occupational Health Advisers who can carry out risk assessments. The assessment should:

- **refer to industry standards (for example, for furniture, equipment or software) where these are relevant to the job or individual concerned**
- **review job-related risk assessments and their implementation to ensure they are valid and effective**
- **be prepared to review if any changes have taken place subsequently affecting the individual job or post-holder**
- **never make assumptions about what constitutes 'light work' or 'heavy work', or about the nature and degree of 'force' or 'exertion' involved in particular jobs**

Always consult the individual when carrying out assessments. They may not always recognise work-related symptoms or causes but will know problems in the workplace.
If an employee has an impairment, they will know how the disability affects them and their ability to do the job and may know the necessary adjustments. Avoid making blanket assumptions about the job or an individual's impairment – objectivity, facts and individual assessments in relation to the actual requirements of particular jobs are essential.

If the solutions are not straightforward or obvious, consider getting advice and assistance from experts such as ergonomists, medical specialists or other occupational health professionals such as physiotherapists, chiropractors, or osteopaths. In selecting your advisors, make sure they have the necessary expertise and understand the full implications of the DDA.

Ergonomic assessment

Ergonomics plays an important role in the prevention and amelioration of upper limb disorders. It is a multi-disciplinary science that inter-relates information from engineering, medicine and psychology: the principle is to design work to be compatible with human limitations and capability. It is important to all environments, from working on an assembly line, at a machine on the factory floor, in meat and poultry preparation, sitting at a computer terminal or behind the wheel of a vehicle. Designing tasks, equipment and workstations to suit the user can reduce errors, accidents and ill-health and will make work more comfortable and productive.

2.12

Ergonomic consultants assess the individual in their working environment. They ensure a good "fit" between employees, the tools they use and the work they do. The Health and Safety Executive (HSE) strongly recommends that employers seek advice from ergonomists when carrying out risk assessments under the Management of Health and Safety at Work Regulations. A full assessment should include consideration of:

- **job design – the actual requirements of the particular job and tasks**
- **working methods, posture, effort and forces involved**
- **equipment and tools (especially hand tools involving gripping action)**
- **work organisation and systems of work, including the variety and allocation of tasks, scheduling of rest breaks, and job rotation**
- **pacing, intensity and duration of work activities**
- **workstations and the work environment (including lighting, noise levels, temperature and ventilation, and the physical features of the premises)**
- **employment arrangements and organisational issues, such as: disability and equality policies; health and safety arrangements and procedures (including risk management and reporting procedures); employment policies and procedures; communications, organisational culture and attitudes, and related management and staff training**

Making reasonable adjustments

In making reasonable adjustments for people with upper limb disorders or repetitive strain injury, flexibility is the key and can often produce more options for employee and employer alike.

The duty to make adjustments also applies to temporary and contract staff as well as employees, so it is important to consider all those affected, in all types of jobs. Adjustments may either be needed temporary or long-term (for example, a transfer to alternative duties).

The process may also involve changes to how other people work, especially if teamwork is involved.

Examples of adjustments

Examples of adjustments relevant to people with upper limb disorders include:

Modifying job design can remove hazards in manual tasks; reduce repetition and vary, alternate or rotate tasks or jobs (e.g. within a team or department); avoid reaching or working with arms raised above elbow height, or other awkward postures such as twisting or bending; avoid static work in a fixed or rigid position.

Modifying equipment:

general: ensure conformity with minimum standards in work equipment, furniture and software; ensure that all equipment is well-maintained and that equipment failures are minimised; make sure that in making an adjustment in one area you are not creating a problem or risk in another

hand tools: redesign hand grips (a wide grip can impose severe strain especially on those with small hands); bend tools and controls rather than the wrist; avoid tools requiring high hand forces, or handles which dig into the palm (spread the load over the largest area); consider using power tools or automation; avoid vibration in hand tools, or provide protection from it where it is unavoidable

control panels: avoid displays where the user has to bend or stretch to see them properly; ensure that both the control panel and the emergency stop button are easy to reach for someone with upper limb disorders, and that they can work comfortably; provide height-adjustable chairs, workbenches, footstools, etc

computer-based adjustments: detailed practical guidance on working with display screen equipment, relevant standards and workstation assessments is available from the Health and Safety Executive. This includes guidance on software standards and ergonomics. Assuming minimum standards have been met, reasonable adjustments to display screen equipment and workstations could include: voice-activated software and a quiet work environment; alternative or ergonomically designed keyboards; alternative key input devices; ergonomic hand-shaped mouse or alternatives to a mouse; software programmes designed to assist customised scheduling of exercise and rest breaks; reducing equipment failure and/or error rates; improvements and/or adaptations to software design, for example to reduce the number of key strokes, and allowing operator-led rather than software-led pacing of data input and word processing

2.12

The Automobile Association

Sean is a Customer Adviser whose role is to take calls from customers and amend their records via a computer terminal. When he complained of pain and discomfort in his hands and wrists, the AA arranged for their Occupational Health Adviser to visit. She recommended frequent breaks, a wrist support, a specially designed chair, and voice activated software and that he visit his GP. Sean's GP referred him to a Consultant Rheumatologist who confirmed a diagnosis of "work related upper limb disorder". In the meantime, the AA called in the PACT (now Disability Service Team) who loaned Sean a Microsoft Natural Keyboard on trial. This proved very useful and the AA purchased one at a cost of £45. In addition, the Occupational Health Adviser's recommendations were implemented. The latest report from the Consultant state that Sean's symptoms have improved following a course of exercises and the workplace adjustments. The AA says: "Sean has been able to carry out the full range of his duties with fairly minor adjustments. We will continue to monitor his progress".

Government Department

Roy is a Policy Advisor in the DfEE (now DWP). In 1996, whilst drafting the DDA employment Code of Practice, Roy began to experience aches, then pains in his left wrist and thumb. His GP referred him to a consultant, who diagnosed a form of RSI (tenosynovitis). As a result, he wore a wrist splint to limit movement, underwent a period of physiotherapy and reduced the amount of keyboard work and heavy lifting. Gradually the pain went. He still wears the splint whilst typing, and the problem has not recurred. Roy says: "My line managers have been very helpful in making reasonable adjustments, providing me with a mousemat with a wrist support, time off for physiotherapy and fully adjustable arms on my chair which allow me to adopt a good typing position.
I have also been made more aware of our telephone dictation system and voice-activated software"

Making other adjustments to employers' premises

Employees with upper limb disorders may be at a substantial disadvantage in accessing employers' premises, including welfare facilities, storage and meeting rooms. Examples of reasonable adjustments here include:

- **access and exit: ensure that doors, handles and locks can be used by everyone: reduce the weight of doors; redesign and/or reposition handles and locks; consider the use of electronic key cards instead of traditional locks, or electronically activated doors; consider all areas,**

including welfare facilities, meeting rooms and other common parts

- **storage arrangements: redesign or relocate storage areas and/or provide alternatives, or provide assistance in accessing these; avoid storage involving heights, especially when combined with reaching, lifting or gripping movements, or twisting and bending to reach them; reduce the weight of filing drawers and file contents, or replace with file carousels or electronic files; provide lifting or load-bearing equipment or assistance when objects need to be carried or moved from one place to another**

- **temperature, ventilation and air-conditioning systems: poorly designed workplace ventilation and air-conditioning systems, draughts and cold, create difficulties for people with upper limb disorders. Adjustments include redesigning these systems, or relocating workstations, so that staff are not seated directly under draughts, and electrical or electronic equipment is still kept cool**

Developing management policies and procedures – a summary

Address issues flexibly and systematically -conduct assessments and introduce changes and adjustments as part of an ongoing systematic review of work methods and organisation – ensure they do not create new problems elsewhere.

Start by consulting the individual. Then seek suitably qualified professional advice when carrying out assessments under the DDA. Appoint a competent person to carry out health and safety risk assessments; ensure that these assessments are monitored, reviewed and revised where necessary.

Ensure that recruitment, selection and appraisal procedures avoid unfair discrimination – adjust aptitude tests and criteria for selection or appraisal to allow everyone to demonstrate abilities in relation to the essential requirements of the specific job in different ways. (This also applies to promotion and transfer, job descriptions, job evaluation criteria and performance-related pay systems, check that these do not discriminate unfairly against disabled people with upper limb disorders).

Where people are new to the work or to equipment, allow a graduated build up to full pace of work and monitor this; where teamwork is involved, consider team-based adjustments: redesign team-working arrangements or reallocate tasks within the team.

Provide training to all concerned on working methods and posture, how to use furniture, tools and equipment correctly, and the importance of rest breaks.

Provide training, information, instruction and supervision in relation to any adjustments, not only to the disabled postholder but also to co-workers and line managers; ensure that others (including professional advisers) understand the reasons for adjustments and are encouraged to view them as positive and constructive measures for everyone.

Develop reporting procedures which encourage and facilitate early reporting of any problems or pain, so that preventive measures can be put in place without delay. Ensure that early reporting is not seen (rightly or wrongly) as a fast track to dismissal or redundancy.

2.12

Adjustments for medical treatment: individuals can have difficulty getting to see appropriate specialists for independent assessment, diagnosis or treatment, especially in certain parts of the country – avoid inflexible pre-set timescales or inflexible limits on the number of treatments available or timing of such treatments.

Allow flexible working patterns – for example: time off for treatment; adjustments in working time to permit a self-paced workload or graduated return to work; flexible working hours or shift patterns; working from home for part or all of the time.

Allow flexible transport and travel arrangements: Employees with upper limb disorders or RSI may also be substantially disadvantaged in relation to the arrangements they make for getting to and from the workplace at particular times, or travelling between different sites, especially if they have to transport equipment or documents. Reasonable adjustments here include:

- **adjusting work times so that rush-hour travel can be avoided**
- **providing assistance with alternative means of transport**
- **ensuring that car leasing or pooled car arrangements are flexible**
- **provide vehicles with adaptations, and with power steering and/or automatic transmission**

If, after all possible, reasonable adjustments, the employee is still unable to perform their job, the employer must consider relocation to another position.

The business case for adjustments

Removing barriers to employment for people with upper limb disorders and RSI, effective risk assessment and prevention, and reasonable adjustments to assist retention, career development and rehabilitation, are good management practices and make sound business sense:

- **they help attract and retain staff and improve staff morale**
- **they help make work safer, healthier and more productive, avoiding serious injury and ill-health and reducing sickness absence and medical retirement rates**

Failure to act can lead to possible costly legal proceedings and personal injury claims against employers.
Making the necessary adjustments in good time can make a real difference in the workplace - leading to more general improvements which benefit everyone, including customers.

Help, advice and information can be obtained from the following organisations

(Contact details are provided at the back of this book).

- **AbilityNet**
- **Employers' Forum on Disability**
- **The Ergonomics Society**
- **The Health and Safety Executive (HSE)**
- **Jobcentre Plus**
- **RSI Association**
- **The Society of Occupational Medicine**

A PRACTICAL GUIDE TO

employment adjustments for people with diabetes

Diabetes, the facts; Definition

Adjustments; Shiftwork; Health and safety concerns

Professional assessments

Diabetes and driving

Restricted occupations

2.13

The Act defines a disabled person as someone with a physical or mental impairment which has a substantial and long-term adverse effect on his ability to carry out normal day-to-day activities. The effects of medical treatment must be disregarded when assessing the impact of a person's disability. Many people with diabetes will qualify for protection under the DDA, even if the individual concerned does not consider himself to be disabled. People with diabetes represent a significant resource in the labour market and at work their talents are often under utilised. People with diabetes may require reasonable adjustments within the workplace - adjustments which are often simple and inexpensive.

Diabetes, the facts

The vast majority of people with diabetes have no problems at work; the employer may not even be aware that they have diabetes. However, for some people, a few minor adjustments may need to be made.

Medically known as "Diabetes mellitus" - diabetes affects approximately 3 per cent of the population. A further 3 per cent may have diabetes and not be aware of it. Although not curable, diabetes can be successfully treated by controlling the level of glucose in the blood. This can be achieved through a regimen of exercise and diet, and – where necessary – oral medication or insulin injections. With correct treatment, most people experience very few practical problems. However, some people do experience long term complications.

Diabetes is often feared and misunderstood. Decisions about suitability for employment, promotion or retention are too often based on general assumptions or misconceptions, rather than a factual assessment. This can lead to discrimination against existing, or potential employees.

Definition

In a person with diabetes there is either a deficiency in the amount of insulin produced, or the body's ability to use it.

2.13

There are two main types of diabetes. In Type 1 diabetes, (previously known as Insulin Dependent Diabetes Mellitus), the body produces no insulin itself, and the diabetes is controlled by insulin injections. Type 2 diabetes, (previously known as Non-Insulin Dependent Diabetes Mellitus), is treated mainly through oral medication and diet, although insulin injections may sometimes be required. Type 1 diabetes, is common in childhood and accounts for roughly 10% of all cases. Type 2 diabetes generally occurs in adulthood and accounts for approximately 85% of all cases.

Hypo / Hyper

Diabetic Hypoglycaemia and Hyperglycaemia, or being "hypo" or "hyper", are terms that you will often hear in relation to diabetes.

Hypoglycaemia

Hypoglycaemia may occur at work. It happens when levels of glucose in the blood become too low due to excess insulin, from treatment, medication, lack of food or too much physical activity. Hypoglycaemia occurs rapidly over several minutes and can be resolved equally as rapidly. Symptoms of hypoglycaemia include confusion, shakiness, weakness, faintness, tiredness, sweating, headache, blurred vision, unsteadiness and hunger. The individual may need to take small amounts of sugar, sweet juice or food containing sugar, followed up with longer lasting starchy carbohydrate, such as a sandwich.

Hyperglycaemia

Hyperglycaemia is unlikely to occur at work. It happens when levels of glucose in the blood become too high due to insufficient insulin or insulin resistance. The onset of hyperglycaemia is gradual, occurring over a period of several days and is very unlikely to develop into an emergency situation at work. Symptoms include excessive thirst, dry mouth & frequent urination. The individual may need extra medication and must monitor his condition carefully. If left untreated, hyperglycaemia can potentially be very dangerous.

Most people with diabetes recognise these symptoms and will take the appropriate action. However, should loss of consciousness occur, emergency services should be called.

Associated conditions

Good control lessens the likelihood of complications. However, some people with diabetes do experience long-term complications. These complications are very slow in onset and generally develop over a period of many years, such as:

- **nerve damage - caused by prolonged high glucose levels -numbness/ tingling in feet and cramps**
- **kidney problems**
- **heart disease**
- **circulation problems in the legs**
- **damage to the eyes, which if left untreated, can result in blindness**

Case study
Greater Manchester Police

Terry Lomax is an inspector with the GMP. He was diagnosed with Type 1 (insulin dependent) diabetes in 1971 when he was a constable with just three years service. He says: "I thought that this would be an abrupt end to a short, but promising career. However, my fears were unfounded. Although police officers are not currently protected by the DDA, my managers and colleagues have been fully supportive throughout my service. As a constable I worked alongside my colleagues on foot patrol, panda car and van duties and worked shifts. I managed my diet and insulin injections whilst remaining an active and efficient police officer."
On promotion to sergeant, he worked both in a busy inner city area as a uniform patrol supervisor and with the CID. As an inspector in one of the busiest cities in the country, he managed about thirty officers. He was involved in typical policing incidents and not so typical incidents like the Strangeways prison riot. He now has 31 years police service and works at the Force Headquarters in the Personnel Branch.
He says: "In the last fourteen years I have had no absences due to sickness. This is an exceptional attendance record rarely matched by my 'fully fit' colleagues."

Adjustments

2.13

Each person's experience of diabetes will be different. People with diabetes have the same goals and aspirations as other employees. Employers should not assume that diabetes will mean an increased Health and Safety risk. Each job should be risk assessed to determine whether there are in fact any significant Health and Safety risks. The individual's medical condition should then be considered in relation to the overall risk assessment to determine whether there are, in fact, any increased risks either to themselves or their colleagues.

Health and Safety regulations require employers to make reasonably practicable adjustments to eliminate or reduce Health & Safety risks. Where a possible concern is identified, the employer, employee and where necessary a "disability expert", can work together to resolve any potential difficulty through either reasonable adjustments under the DDA, or reasonably practicable adjustments under Health and Safety legislation. If job duties change, new adjustments may be required.

2.13

In most cases, the only reasonable adjustment required is an increased understanding of diabetes by those in the workplace. It is very important to involve the individual concerned when considering or making ANY reasonable adjustment. In some cases, consideration could be given to:

- **staff awareness training**
- **regular work schedules, breaks and meal breaks – a predictable routine may be vital to those who need to monitor their glucose levels, take insulin or eat**
- **somewhere (fridge, insulated cool bag, wide mouth flask) to store insulin if necessary**
- **private space for testing blood glucose levels and or injecting insulin if required**
- **allowing time off to attend medical appointments, rehabilitation or assessments**
- **allowing the individual to gradually build up the level of fitness required**
- **reallocation of duties**
- **relocation to alternative position/employment/premises**
- **establish procedures for dealing with a hypoglycaemic attack, in conjunction with the individual**
- **(where there is a diabetes related visual impairment) appropriate lighting, large print (for training materials, application forms etc.), use of adaptive equipment, performing tasks in a different manner (see Chapter 2.7: 'Employment adjustments for people with visual impairments')**

Case study
QinetiQ

Lyndon Rodway has been employed by QinetiQ for the last 21 years. He was diagnosed with Type 1 (insulin dependent) diabetes in 1975. He currently works as a Project Support Consultant to the Defence Procurement Agency, providing advice on software purchasing. Problems arose with the considerable amount of time he had to spend away from home whilst working on a specific contract. He says: "Last year I spent over 150 full days, and 100 nights away in hotels. Travelling, overtime and hotel food made it very difficult for me to control when, and what I could eat. As a direct result, I began to experience a deterioration in my eyesight, and kidney problems."

Lyndon advised his line managers and arranged for duties that require him to be away from home for long periods to be reallocated to colleagues. He has spent only 7 nights away in the last 6 months. He says: "As a result of being better able to control my diet, my last visit to the clinic has shown a noticeable improvement in my condition."

Shift work

There is a common misconception that a person with diabetes is unable to work shifts. This belief is often unjustified. Although shift work may create difficulties for some people with diabetes, an individual whose diabetes is well controlled may experience no difficulties at all. Again, it is important to assess each case on its own merits, not to make assumptions and to work with the individual to overcome any difficulties.

DDA Case
Jones v National Standard Co. Ltd.
1304313/97

Mr Jones has diabetes. He was originally employed as a 'checker' in a factory. However, when the employers cut production there was less need for 'checkers' and Mr Jones was offered a job as a 'rewinder' as an alternative to redundancy. He took the new job on a trial basis. He was required to top up tanks of acid and caustic soda. This was contrary to previous advice by the company doctor that he should not work near the tanks in case he became hypoglycaemic and fainted. Mr Jones raised the problem with the production control manager, who asked for volunteers to switch jobs with Mr Jones. When no one came forward, Mr Jones was dismissed.

The tribunal found that the employers were unaware of the DDA. They had given no thought to reasonable adjustments. Specifically, the tribunal said that they should have considered reallocating the job of refilling the acid and caustic soda tanks, a small part of the duties , to another employee. They had also given inadequate attention to the possibility of alternative employment. There was no justification for the course which the employers had followed. The dismissal was unfair and amounted to unlawful discrimination under the DDA.

2.13

Health and Safety concerns

Situations may arise where employers believe they cannot meet their statutory duties under health and safety law if they employ a person with diabetes in a particular job. However, if an employer refuses to employ or retain a person with diabetes and the reasons are ill founded, this may lead to the employer being taken to tribunal under the DDA. Where Health and Safety is put forward as the reason for refusal to employ an individual, be sure that the reason is justifiable, given the facts regarding a particular person in a specific job, and cannot be resolved by reasonable adjustments. (See Chapter 1.4: 'Health and Safety & the DDA')

Professional Assessments

Employers need to have a professional assessment of the control an individual may have over their diabetes. This is an important consideration for occupations

2.13

with inherent hazards, for example:

- **working with chemicals, unguarded fires, ovens and hotplates**
- **working with unguarded machinery**
- **working with high voltage or open circuit electricity**
- **working near open water**
- **working on or near moving vehicles**
- **working at unprotected heights**

Treatments used to control diabetes, may place restrictions upon, or deny the individual access to, certain occupations. Restrictions will vary according to the individual's diabetes and how it is controlled:

- **diet alone:** if there are no significant and disabling complications, there are no statutory occupational restrictions
- **oral medication and diet:** few occupational limitations, providing there are no disabling complications. Restrictions apply within some of the occupations listed, although these may differ according to whether the condition was diagnosed whilst 'in service'
- **insulin:** for reasons of health & safety, statutory restrictions apply. Hypoglycaemia through excess insulin, too little food or excessive physical activity can result in a rapid loss of control or consciousness which would make certain occupations hazardous

Restricted occupations

There are restrictions on the recruitment of people who treat their diabetes with insulin in the following occupations:

- **armed forces**
- **airline pilot *****
- **jobs requiring a Large Goods Vehicle (LGV over 7.5 tonnes), or a Passenger Carrying Vehicle (PCV over 16 seats) licence *****
- **police and hire service (currently under review)**
- **working off-shore, e.g. on oil-rigs or cruise liners, regardless of the type of job *****
- **train driving, or working near/on a railway track *****
- **working at heights**

*** This indicates the occupations where employees will be transferred to alternative duties or medically dismissed at point when diabetes becomes treated with insulin.

Case study
London Fire Brigade

Tim Hoy has been in the fire service for 14 years. In 1989, he was diagnosed with Type 1 (insulin dependent) diabetes. He was immediately removed from operational firefighting and became a recruitment trainer. He won an appeal against medical retirement and was reinstated to full operational duties. Tim says: "When I was diagnosed, I thought it heralded the end of my career. My knowledge of diabetes at that time was extremely limited and, due to my ignorance, what I did know was all highly negative. This level of ignorance is sadly commonplace, and the employment world often does a great disservice to highly motivated and capable people who are merely different."

Of attitudes he says: "Once educated, I never considered my diabetes to be an issue. What I did find disabling however, was other peoples attitudes towards my wholly controllable medical condition. It was after all, other people's beliefs rather than any difficulty I experienced that had excluded me from doing my job."

Tim founded the International Register of Firefighters with Diabetes in 1991. Although firefighters are not currently protected by the DDA, there are at least 55 fully operational fighters with diabetes in the UK.

Diabetes and driving

From 1991, people treated with insulin are not generally allowed to hold licences to drive 'Group 2 vehicles' – Large Goods Vehicles (above 7.5 tonnes) or vehicles with more than 16 seats.

In 1996, with limited exceptions the Group 2 definition was extended to include vehicles weighing 3.5–7.5 tonnes (category C1) and vehicles with 9–16 seats (category D1). Modifications relating to C1 vehicles were made to the regulations in 1998 and again in 2001. The result is that from 5 April 2001, licence applicants who use insulin are allowed to drive these medium-sized vehicles provided they meet certain prescribed medical criteria (i.e. individual assessment). Licences must be renewed annually.

Licences for Group 1 vehicles (e.g. a family car) continue to be renewed on a 1, 2, or more usually 3 year basis.

For further information regarding diabetes and driving, contact Diabetes UK. Individuals that do not use insulin as treatment are not affected by this legislation.

Help, advice and information can be obtained from the following organisations

(Contact details are provided at the back of this book).

- **Diabetes UK**
- **Davies Associates**
- **Employers' Forum on Disability**
- **I.R.F.D. (International Register of Firefighters with Diabetes)**
- **Jobcentre Plus**

A PRACTICAL GUIDE TO

employment adjustments for people with epilepsy

Epilepsy, the facts; definition

Adjustments, health and safety concerns

Restricted occupations

2.14

Approximately 300,000 people in the UK have a form of epilepsy. However, although epilepsy is the second most common neurological condition in the UK, much fear and lack of knowledge surrounds the condition.

This section provides practical advice and guidance to employers who already employ, or wish to employ a person with epilepsy. It can also be given to employees, who in discussion with their employer, can help identify their particular needs and adopt solutions which improve the working environment.

In researching this section, it became very clear that most people with epilepsy require very few adjustments. Disability awareness and keeping an open mind may be the only adjustments necessary. An employee with epilepsy will usually know what is required, so contact and consultation with the employee is vital.

Epilepsy – the facts

- **the vast majority of people with epilepsy have no problems at work; the employer may not even be aware that the person has epilepsy**
- **epilepsy can affect anyone at any age; if no one in your workforce presently has epilepsy it is more than likely that someone will in the future.**
- **people with epilepsy will have the same goals and aspirations as any other employee**
- **each person's experience of epilepsy is different**

According to the National Society for Epilepsy, approximately 100 people are diagnosed with epilepsy each day. There are many kinds of epilepsy, each having different effects. Although 1 in

20 people experience a seizure at some point in their lives, epilepsy is the tendency to experience recurring seizures. At least 1 in 200 people have epilepsy in the UK.

Approximately 80 per cent of people with epilepsy have complete control over their seizures with medication. Some people may have some side effects however, particularly when they first start taking medication.

2.14

Case Study – From Forum Information Helpline

Query:
An organisation recruited an individual who had epilepsy. On her application form and at the interview stage, she declared that her epilepsy was under control and that she had not experienced a seizure for more than a year. However, within the first two weeks she had numerous seizures. The case was referred to the Occupational Health Adviser who said that she must have lied about the status of her epilepsy during the recruitment procedure. At this point the employer did not know what to do and called for advice.

Reply:
There were several issues to consider here:

- **it does not necessarily follow that she lied about her epilepsy. Many factors can trigger seizures, including stress, anxiety, tiredness, starting a new job, shift work or factors in the workplace such as flickering lights. Medication that previously controlled her epilepsy may have become ineffective or she may be taking new medication. She may simply need time for her doctors to assess what new medication is going to be effective in controlling the seizures**

- **it is vital that the employer talks to her about her epilepsy. These discussions should be handled sensitively. She should be reassured that she is not being disciplined, or the stress could trigger further seizures**

- **the employer should ask the employee if any reasonable adjustments would help her. These could include time off until her medication is reassessed and/or until new medication is effective. If she remains at work, she should be encouraged to tell someone when a seizure is imminent. This may not be possible for people who do not have a warning, or have a very short warning. As a reasonable adjustment she could be provided with the use of a quiet room to which she can go if she feels a seizure coming on. It may also be appropriate for someone who works with her to be trained to take first aid action when she has a seizure**

- **Occupational Health should ask for her permission to gain medical reports from her GP and in particular from her specialist regarding her previous and current situation and to obtain a prognosis**
- **the employer should call in the Disability Service Teams (DSTs), at the local Jobcentre. The DSTs can assess the workplace and give advice on further reasonable adjustments**

Definition

Epilepsy is a generic term used to describe the tendency to have recurrent seizures. Seizures occur when there is a momentary disturbance in the electrochemical activity of the brain. Sometimes this will also affect the brain's control of the body. A seizure will generally last no more than a few seconds or minutes after which the brain cells will return to their normal state. Most people do not experience any ill effects once the seizure has finished; some may need a short recovery period.

Epilepsy occurs in many different forms. Some seizures are easily recognised, whereas others are less obvious. Just knowing that an employee or potential employee has epilepsy is not very helpful and provides very little useful information. The four main types are:

- **tonic-clonic seizure (formerly called grand mal). The person may have rigid and jerky movements of the body. Usually lasts for a few minutes**
- **absence seizure. The person may just unknowingly stare. Usually lasts for a few seconds**
- **simple partial seizure. The person experiences strange feelings in one part of the body, for example loss of hearing**
- **complex partial seizure. The person may not be aware of their surroundings and may behave out of character**

2.14

Usually consciousness is only lost during a tonic-clonic seizure. The key action points when someone loses consciousness when experiencing a seizure are simple first aid procedures:

- **do not try to move or restrain the person**
- **do not try to wake them**
- **loosen any tight clothing around their neck, if possible**
- **cushion their head**
- **move any objects that may cause injury**
- **stay with them until they recover**
- **call an ambulance only if they have injured themselves, fail to regain consciousness after about 5 minutes,**

or if they have another seizure without regaining consciousness

- **when the person regains consciousness they may be confused and may need to be reassured or helped to a quiet room to recover**

Your first aiders should be fully aware of this process. The employee should be asked to advise you if they have any particular requirements, and if they carry a medical alert card or bracelet.

2.14 Photosensitive or light sensitive epilepsy and VDUs

Photosensitive epilepsy can be triggered by flickering light, either natural or artificial. Very few people with epilepsy have photosensitive epilepsy. Although someone with photosensitive epilepsy is most likely to have a tonic-clonic seizure, the person could experience any type of seizure.

People often assume that VDUs will cause a problem for people who have photosensitive epilepsy, however this is not normally the case. VDUs usually operate at a high frequency that will not provoke seizures. However, there are cases of people with this rare type of epilepsy who experience seizures, triggered by such things as VDUs, TVs, monitor screens, low frequency or flashing light, bright glaring light, stripes or checks. It is always best not to assume the cause of a seizure but to be guided by the person. Often they will have identified what triggers a seizure and adopted coping strategies, for example wearing dark glasses in bright light or covering one eye if exposed to flashing or flickering light.

Photosensitive or light sensitive epilepsy is more common, although still rare, among children and adolescents. As it becomes less frequent with age, working age people are less likely to be affected.

Case Study – Inland Revenue

Ann has worked for the Inland Revenue for almost 30 years. She has photosensitive epilepsy and a sight impairment which she acquired in her early forties after a serious accident. Considering herself lucky to be alive, and too young to retire, Ann returned to work in a new position.
She openly discussed her epilepsy with colleagues and others with whom she came into contact, both to protect herself and reassure them in the event of a tonic-clonic seizure.
Her employer values the work she has done to improve their services to disabled customers; she has been responsible for the disability awareness and training of the entire workforce of around 74,000 people. Currently, she is reviewing all human resources processes and procedures to ensure the Inland Revenue becomes a leading example of a best practice employer of disabled people.

Because of her epilepsy and visual impairment, Ann has been "lucky" enough to recieve her own office where she has access to natural light. Lighting has also been changed in the women's toilet and the reception area. She wears dark glasses when she goes out in bright light. Ann has the use of a personal secretary (provided both as an adjustment and because of her grade) who accesses technology for her, including e-mail and the Intranet, reformats text in large print and photocopies which Ann cannot do because of the flashing screens. When she attends events, Ann notifies the organisers and tells them of her epilepsy so adjustments can be made.

If presentations involve overhead projections, she can look away and listen instead.

Ann states, 'I'm passionate about my job and know that with the right sort of support and understanding from managers and colleagues I can make a real difference. I may have to do things differently because of my disabilities but I can do them just as well'.

Health and Safety concerns

Under the Health & Safety at Work Act 1974 both employers and employees have a duty of care to maintain a safe working environment. Where relevant, a person with epilepsy has a duty to inform their employer so that responsibilities under the 1974 act can be fulfilled. However, employers should not just assume that epilepsy will mean an increased health and safety risk as this will not usually be the case.

Each job should be assessed to determine whether there are any significant health and safety risks. Where a possible concern is identified, the employer, employee, and where necessary a Disability Employment Adviser (contactable through your local Jobcentre) and an Occupational Health practitioner, can work together to minimise or remove the risks through adjustments. If job duties change, new adjustments may be required.

Situations may arise whereby employers believe they cannot meet their statutory duties under health and safety law if they employ a person with epilepsy in a particular job. However, if an employer refuses to employ or retain a person with epilepsy and the reasons are ill founded, this may lead to the employer being taken to tribunal under the DDA. You should avoid blanket exclusions.

For more information on health and safety, see Chapter 1.4: 'A practical guide to Health and Safety & the DDA'.

Holmes v Whittingham & Porter

Mr Holmes worked as a labourer for Whittingham & Porter for 31 years, during which he had epilepsy and occasional seizures with robotic movements. On the one and only occasion when he collapsed during a seizure his employer suspended him while awaiting a report from his GP. This report was sent to the employer's medical adviser, who the tribunal noted was neither a specialist in occupational medicine or epilepsy. The employer's medical adviser expressed concern that part of Mr Holmes' job involved walking around the factory where there was hot metal and forging hammers and that he might be a danger to himself and others. After a meeting with Mr Holmes to discuss this advice, the employer dismissed Mr Holmes.

The tribunal noted that if Mr Holmes had not had epilepsy he would not have been dismissed. Mr Holmes had been treated less favourably for a reason related to his disability and the question therefore remained 'can the employer justify this?' The tribunal held that it could not, because its medical adviser was inadequately qualified, not having any particular knowledge of epilepsy. An epilepsy specialist might have been able to suggest change in medication, or an occupational health specialist could have considered adjustments. The employer had not really given Mr Holmes any time to see whether the seizure recurred in this form.

The compensation that the tribunal awarded to Mr Holmes included the sum of £4,250 for injury to feelings, as he had been admitted to hospital for depression following his dismissal.

Adjustments

Employers lose good employees due to their lack of knowledge about epilepsy and its impact in the workplace.

Part of the solution is not to make decisions based on assumptions. Many people with epilepsy face discrimination through misinformation, misunderstanding, ignorance and fear. As a result people with epilepsy often have under-utilised skills. Seek to establish the facts from the individual, or where necessary from medical professionals and consider the person's particular situation before deciding whether there will be limitations. Remember that 80 per cent of people with epilepsy have complete control of their seizures through medication. As a further example, someone may have seizures during their sleep and as such may be unlikely to experience any seizures during their working day.

In most cases, the only reasonable adjustment required is your increased awareness and an acceptance of people who have epilepsy by colleagues in the workplace. It is very important to involve the individual when considering or making ANY reasonable adjustment. Adjustments should be considered in light of their specific job. Do not impose blanket restrictions on everyone with a disability or a particular type of disability such as epilepsy. Consider when you are assessing the need for adjustments:

- **is the epilepsy controlled?**
- **are there any before or after effects?**
- **does the employee know when a seizure is imminent?**
- **does stress, anxiety or tiredness induce seizures?**
- **does anything specific trigger a seizure?**
- **is there a pattern of seizures?**
- **is there any specific care that should be given either during or after a seizure?**
- **what are the frequency, duration and type of seizures?**
- **what is the usual recovery time?**

The employer should consider adjustments:

- **allow time off for medical treatment**
- **be flexible wherever possible around working hours and work loads**
- **be aware that medication or epilepsy itself, may occasionally affect memory, concentration or mood**
- **be flexible when allowing an individual to adapt to a new treatment regime**
- **if the person wishes, ensure all staff are given awareness training on epilepsy, or ensure that epilepsy is covered as a matter of course in any disability awareness session**
- **provide a safe, comfortable place for the individual to have a seizure or recover**
- **allow the person to have more frequent breaks from looking at a computer screen**
- **use ordinary, as opposed to fluorescent tube lighting which flickers (at a high frequency) – this should be considered as a general workplace issue anyway to ensure a healthy environment**

2.14

Calvert v Jewelglen Ltd

Mr Calvert, an experienced care assistant, was employed by a nursing home as a care assistant. He declared that he had epilepsy, and that due to his medication regime, he had remained seizure free for the last eighteen years. Only senior management were aware of his medical history and were happy to employ him.

As a side effect of his medication he often experienced dizzy spells which would pass very rapidly. However, on one occasion a dizzy spell persisted and he reported it to the Night Sister who sent him home. She was previously unaware of his epilepsy. Based on assumptions and without any investigation, she told him that he was not required and that he was

2.14

to call the owner who might relocate him to a clerical position. However, on speaking to the owner it became apparent that he was not prepared to employ Mr. Calvert at all. Mr Calvert was dismissed purely on the basis of the Night Sister's concerns without any further investigation. The reason given for his dismissal was his past medical history, and the amount of sedatives he was currently prescribed.

The Tribunal held that Mr Calvert was disabled under the remit of the DDA and that his dismissal was not justified, as the decision to dismiss was taken without further investigation of the Night Sister's concerns, or proper inquiry as to the real facts. The tribunal awarded a total of £6,940 compensation, including £2,500 for injury to feelings. £100 was also awarded for aggravated damages 'by reason of the manner in which he was handled and the way in which the dismissal was carried out'.

Driving Regulations

Some people with epilepsy can, and do, hold valid driving licenses. However, anyone who experiences a seizure must not drive until:

- **they have been 'seizure free' for 12 months**
- **OR they have experienced sleep seizures only, for at least 3 years**
- **AND the Driving and Vehicle Licensing Agency (DVLA) is satisfied the person is not likely to be a danger on the road**

To obtain an LGV, HGV or PCV licence, the person must have been seizure free, without taking anti-epileptic medication, for the last 10 years. The DVLA also need to be satisfied that there is no likelihood that the person will have further seizures.

The regulations encompass ALL seizure types including auras/warnings and where consciousness is not impaired. If a person remains free of seizures for 7 years, they may be entitled to hold a full licence that is valid until they are 70. In all cases information from their GP is required.

For more details on driving regulations, contact the Driving and Vehicle Licensing Agency (DVLA).

When drawing up job descriptions it is important not simply to assume that a driving licence is required, as this may discriminate against disabled people. The employer should consider whether driving is an essential part of the job. Reasonable adjustments under the DDA include:

- **driving allocated to someone else**
- **the need to drive waived. Alternative means of transport should be considered, including taxis**

Restricted occupations

There are statutory provisions preventing people with a history of epilepsy joining the following professions.

- **air traffic controller**
- **aircraft pilot**
- **ambulance driver (need to be free from seizures for at least 10 years)**
- **fire-fighter**
- **prison officer**
- **train driver**

There are other professions where restrictions may apply depending on such factors as the length of time a person has been free of seizures, the control of seizures, or where there may be a substantial risk, for example:

- **airline cabin staff**
- **armed services**
- **divers**
- **merchant navy**
- **some teaching posts in state schools**
- **working near open water**
- **working at unprotected heights**
- **working alone with babies or young children**
- **working alone on isolated sites**
- **working around unguarded machinery or fires**
- **working on or near moving vehicles**
- **working with high voltage or open circuit electricity**

For more details on restricted occupations contact the British Epilepsy Association or The National Society for Epilepsy.

Help, advice and information can be obtained from the following organisations

(Contact details are provided at the back of this book).

- **British Epilepsy Association**
- **DVLA**
- **Employers' Forum on Disability**
- **Jobcentre Plus**
- **The National Society for Epilepsy**

A PRACTICAL GUIDE TO

employment adjustments for people with back problems

Reasonable adjustments

Health and Safety

Ergonomics

2.15

This section describes some of the adjustments that can be considered for people with back problems. Given that some of these back conditions are work-related, the section takes into account both the adjustments required under the Disability Discrimination Act (DDA) and the risk assessments and ergonomic considerations required under health and safety legislation. Integrated management approaches can then be developed.

The section cannot substitute for specialist advice or assessment in specific cases, and does not cover medical treatment. Sources of further information, specialist advice and assistance are listed for reference at the end of this section.

To prevent back problems leading to lengthy sickness absences, employers should look to make reasonable adjustments as early as possible.

This section should be read in conjunction with Chapter 1.5 – 'A practical guide to managing sickness absence'.

The DDA and back problems

Under the Disability Discrimination Act (1995) it is unlawful for an employer to treat a disabled applicant for a job, or an employee, less favourably for a reason related to their disability, without justification.

People with back problems may not consider themselves to be disabled but they may well be protected by the DDA definition of disability. The DDA definition includes impairments which are likely to recur; this may well include some back problems.

As the effects of medical treatment need to be discounted when assessing whether someone is disabled according to the Act, this will include any painkillers being taken for back pain.

The DDA defines a disabled person as someone with "a physical or mental impairment, which has a substantial and long-term adverse effect" on their ability to carry out normal day-to-day activities. "Long-term" means that it must have lasted, or be expected to last, at least 12 months.

2.15 An employer has a duty under the DDA to make reasonable adjustments to prevent an employee from being placed at a substantial disadvantage by any physical feature of the premises, or by working arrangements. When deciding whether or not an adjustment is reasonable an employer should consider:

- **the effectiveness of the adjustment in preventing the disadvantage**
- **the practicality of the adjustment**
- **the financial and other costs of the adjustment and the extent of any disruption caused**
- **the extent of the employer's financial or other resources**
- **the availability to the employer of financial or other assistance to help make an adjustment, for example through the Access to Work scheme and the support of the Employment Services' Disability Service Teams**

Health and Safety concerns may constitute a reason for less favourable treatment of an employee. However, employers should not automatically assume that Health and Safety issues will supersede the DDA. First, reasonable adjustments should be considered to try to resolve the problem.

It is more prudent to take a positive attitude to resolve problems and make reasonable adjustments, rather than spend time and money trying to establish if someone is technically covered by the Act.

The need to be proactive

The greatest reason for time-off work for ill health is back problems; 12.5% of all sickness absence is related to low back disorders (Andersson 1999). It affects a large number of people and is the leading cause of disability. One fifth of cases brought under the DDA have been related to back problems. According to BackCare:

- **back problems cost the UK £6 billion each year in lost production, benefits and treatment**
- **of the £6 billion cost to the UK economy, £4 billion is due to time-off work**
- **119 million working days are lost each year due to back problems. On average, each person who has back pain and related conditions takes 13 days off work**

- **half the office workers who use a telephone for at least 2 hours a day, and also use a computer, report back pain**

- **after six months absence due to back problems, there is only a 50% chance of someone coming back to work**

- **after a year of absence due to back problems, there is only a 5% chance of someone coming back to work**

- **in two out of three cases, back pain clears up within one month (although re-injury is more likely if risk factors are not corrected)**

As well as absence from work, the costs to organisations which fail to manage back problems efficiently include:

- **reduced performance from staff in pain and discomfort**

- **loss of trained and experienced employees**

- **cost of early ill health retirement**

- **risk of litigation**

It is vital to take a positive and proactive approach to managing back problems in the workplace, so as to minimise back pain related absences and retain good members of staff. You may already have employees who will be covered by the DDA due to back problems; you may also have employees experiencing some discomfort, which if not addressed could lead to future problems and disability. Indeed, poor work practices and stress can lead to members of staff who have never had back problems developing difficulties.

Asking your staff what they find difficult, what problems they have, and reviewing the days that have been lost due to back pain within your organisation will identify the extent of the problem and provide a starting point. This may be carried out through Human Resources. Job tasks, equipment, work environment, and the duration and intensity of work activities will then need to be reassessed to minimise the incidence of back problems being caused by work. This should be done in consultation with specialist assessors, such as ergonomists and Occupational Health practitioners.

Employers should explain to employees that they want to help people recover and encourage early reporting of back pain. If back problems have been identified, arranging treatment and a rehabilitation programme in discussion with the employee may reduce the time off work.

If an employee's absence continues, there may be psychological factors which need to be identified, for example apprehension that the pain may recur, the fear of now not being able to do the job, or anxiety or depression directly related to the back problem.

2.15

Keeping in contact with the employee while they are absent is vital so that they do not feel isolated and are encouraged to return to work.

Case study – AA

The AA, part of the Centrica Group, employs 3,600 patrols. Their work is physically demanding and takes them out in all weathers, often in difficult situations, whether repairing cars at the roadside, fixing vehicles on the hard shoulders of motorways, or attending road traffic accidents.

The AA's Occupational Health Department adopts a proactive approach to health issues. Those who drive receive full screening which ensures that issues are picked up at an early stage and dealt with before any conditions render the patrol incapable of carrying out duties.

As musculoskeletal problems constitute 68% of absences and possible termination of contracts, the AA has developed a strong working relationship with Sketchley Hall and Unsted Park. They offer back rehabilitation programmes aimed at getting patrols and other staff back to work. The programmes consist of an initial assessment to ensure that there are no major health problems, and are carried out in conjunction with the employee's GP. The programme consists of hydrotherapy, exercises, and pain management techniques. Last year, 34 out of 35 patrols were rehabilitated back to full duties.

The long term benefits of such a programme are the savings that a company experiences in not having an employee off on long term sickness. The employee also benefits, by being given every assistance with their back pain and the opportunity to return to work.

Who is affected?

Everyone and anyone is at risk from developing back problems. People will particularly be at risk when the job involves lifting loads, repetitive movements or vibrations, or when they have a poor posture. Poor posture may be the result of, or aggravated by, a poorly designed and arranged workstation.

There is a greater risk of back problems in certain occupations, for example:

- **care workers**
- **construction trades**
- **labourers**
- **nursing**
- **sales and shop assistants**

All the above professions demand manual handling. Other professions where there is an above average risk include:

- **call centres**
- **drivers**
- **office workers**

These professions all involve people adopting a static position for many hours of the week.

Case Law – Sandy v Hampshire Constabulary

Mr Sandy suffered a fall when in the army which damaged his back. He also had partial loss of hearing, compensated by implants in his ears. In November 1995 he applied for a temporary Station Enquiry Officer post. He completed a medical report and was given medical clearance. He was employed in this post for 13 and a half months, during which time he had 5 days sickness absence; one for a stomach problem and four for an ear operation.
In December 1996 he applied for a permanent Station Enquiry Officer post at another police station. He was offered the post subject to references and medical clearance. Mr Sandy's GP sent a medical report stating that Mr Sandy took regular Ibuprofen and occasional Paracetomol, that he was only 'troubled in a very intermittent way by back problems' and that he did not anticipate 'any significant problems in the context of the post'.

The Force Medical Officer informed the Occupational Health & Welfare Department that Mr Sandy was unfit for the post, because the physical demands of the job and his back injury, would mean that Mr Sandy would have an unacceptable level of sickness absence, above the national average of seven days and above extra days given as a reasonable adjustment. The Force medical officer also stated that it was not in Mr Sandy's 'best interests as a back pain sufferer to suffer these duties permanently'.

Mr Sandy brought a claim for disability discrimination

The tribunal found that Mr Sandy had been treated less favourably because of his disabilty, as his offer of employment had been withdrawn. This treatment was not justified because the decision not to employ him was not based on his actual sickness abcence records. The assumption that he would take more than the average number of days off sick was arbitrary and speculative and contradicted the advice of Mr Sandy's GP. There was no effort made to examine Mr Sandy or ask him how his condition affected his abilities.

The tribunal noted that the Occupational Health and Welfare Department had not used its own judgement when deciding whether Mr Sandy could be employed.

In light of the size and resources of Hampshire Constabulary, the tribunal noted that it had failed to have any regard for the DDA at all and had therefore discriminated against Mr Sandy.

2.15

Reasonable adjustments – recruitment

You need to make sure you do not discriminate against a disabled job applicant during the recruitment procedure.

You may have to make reasonable adjustments. Equally, an applicant may previously have had a back problem, but have no difficulties now. It is important not to make assumptions about what the applicant can or cannot do. Instead, ask applicants about reasonable adjustments as part of the recruitment procedure.

Make sure that job descriptions and candidate specifications are not vague. If the job involves lifting then make sure that the type of load and weight is specified. You should also generally consider whether:

- **aids, equipment, or training can change the way the lifting is performed**
- **the task can be reallocated within the team if an applicant would have difficulties with the lifting and it is only a small part of the job**

Reasonable adjustments in employment – and preventing back problems

Many of the adjustments you will need to consider for someone with a back problem, will be good practice for every employee and will help reduce the incidence of back problems.

A sedentary lifestyle and poor posture increases the possibility of back problems. You should encourage employees to remain active – to take their break at lunchtime and, if possible, to go for a walk and to take regular exercise.

Good practice recommendations for all employees, including those with existing back problems, to prevent sickness absence will include:

- **training employees how to be aware of risks and how to report them, possibly as part of the induction process, by a designated health and safety officer**
- **headsets for employees who use the telephone frequently – cradling the telephone can lead to neck and back problems**
- **chairs with appropriate back support, at correct height and distance from the desk**
- **computer screen at appropriate height and angle for the person's height**
- **taking breaks from work and moving around during these breaks**
- **regular stretching**

Particular consideration should be given whenever lifting is required. Consider:

- **whether lifting is necessary or appropriate**

For example, if a delivery is made, can it be delivered directly to the area where it will be used rather than employees subsequently having to move it.

- **using aids, equipment, training, or additional support from trained colleagues to change the way the lifting is performed**
- **reducing the weight of loads that need to be carried**
- **job rotation**

Additional adjustments that should be considered for someone experiencing back problems include:

- **reallocating tasks that exacerbate the back problem, for example lifting**
- **allowing time off for a rehabilitation programme, or medical treatment**
- **flexible working hours, so that, for example if a back problem is particularly painful in the morning the employee can start and finish work later**
- **the use of a spare office if an employee needs to lie down at lunchtime and rest their back**
- **part-time working or job-share if the back problem does not make full time work viable**
- **redeployment if the employee can no longer carry out the current job**
- **paying for an employee to visit a medical specialist, for example to see a physiotherapist. If the employee will face a long wait on the NHS and they will benefit from early intervention by a medical specialist, it may benefit the employer to pay for the first few sessions. Otherwise, minor back problems may become more significant**

The legislative framework

Under the Health and Safety at Work Act 1974 (HSWA), employers have a duty to provide, amongst other things, a safe system of work and to "ensure, as far as is reasonably practicable, the health, safety and welfare at work of all employees".

The Management of Health and Safety at Work Regulations 1992 (the "Management Regulations") outline legal duties to assess risks to the health and safety of employees, and others, arising from the work or workplace involved. The Health and Safety at Work Regulations apply to all organisations, regardless of size. (see Chapter 1.4 – 'Health and Safety and the DDA').

Employers must use a competent person to assist them in assessing risks and implementing protective measures (competence involves having the relevant skills, knowledge and experience to undertake the task). Employers must also:

- **make a 'suitable and sufficient' assessment of risks to the person(s) concerned 'in good time'**
- **consult and co-operate with others, including contractors and safety representatives**
- **as far as is reasonably practicable, remove or reduce any risks, including risks to disabled staff and others already in employment**
- **monitor, review and, if necessary, revise preventive measures to ensure they are effective**
- **provide information, instruction, training and supervision for staff**

2.15

Where five or more people are employed, employers are required to record significant findings of risk assessments in writing and identify any groups of workers particularly at risk. The Approved Code of Practice (ACoP) accompanying the Management Regulations refers to disabled staff as one such group. Some people with back problems may be included here. Others may have back problems which could deteriorate to the point where they are included.

These general duties, to assess and control risks to all staff, including those with back problems, are also reflected in specific regulations such as:

- **the Display Screen Equipment Regulations 1992**
- **the Manual Handling Regulations 1992**
- **the Provision and use of Work Equipment Regulations 1998**

The Manual Handling Regulations 1992 require employers to avoid manual handling wherever practical. When avoidance is not practical, the employer has to assess risks to health, including taking into account the capabilities of the person lifting, and take steps to reduce the risks. Additional requirements affecting workplaces and that are also relevant for people with back problems include The Workplace (Health Safety and Welfare) Regulations 1992 and The Working Time Regulations 1998. These recognise, amongst other things, the need to limit or adjust patterns of work and rest to prevent risks to employee health and safety.

Assessment – general principles

Workplace assessments should be built into a rehabilitation programme. The assessments can aid recovery and/or return to work, and prevent recurrence or further disability. Individuals with back problems will naturally vary in age, size, shape and gender, in the way they carry out their jobs, and in the nature and extent of their disability and how it affects them and their work. Assessments must take individual differences and preferences into account, as well as work duties.

Your company may already have an appointed person who carries out risk assessments. If not, The Society of Occupational Medicine has a list of Occupational Health Advisers who can carry out risk assessments. The assessment should:

- **refer to industry standards (for example, for furniture, equipment or software) where these are relevant to the job or individual concerned**
- **review job-related risk assessments and their implementation to ensure they are valid and effective**
- **be prepared to review if any changes have taken place subsequently affecting the individual job or post-holder**
- **never make assumptions about what constitutes 'light work' or 'heavy work', or about the nature and degree of 'force' or 'exertion' involved in particular jobs**

Always consult the individual when carrying out assessments. They may not always recognise work-related symptoms or causes but will know problems in the workplace. If an employee has an impairment, they will know how the disability affects them and their ability to do the job and may know the necessary adjustments. Avoid making blanket assumptions about the job or an individual's impairment – objectivity, facts and individual assessments in relation to the actual requirements of particular jobs are essential.

If the solutions are not straightforward or obvious, consider getting advice and assistance from experts such as ergonomists, medical specialists or other occupational health professionals such as physiotherapists, chiropractors, or osteopaths. In selecting your advisors, make sure they have the necessary expertise and understand the full implications of the DDA.

Ergonomics

2.15

Ergonomic consultants assess the individual in their working environment. They ensure a good "fit" between employees, the tools they use and the work they do. The Health and Safety Executive (HSE) strongly recommends that employers seek advice from ergonomists when carrying out risk assessments under the Management of Health and Safety at Work Regulations. A full assessment should include consideration of:

- **job design - the actual requirements of the particular job and tasks involved**
- **working methods, posture, effort and forces involved**
- **equipment and tools (especially hand tools involving gripping action)**
- **work organisation and systems of work, including the variety and allocation of tasks, scheduling of rest breaks, and job rotation**

- pacing, intensity and duration of work activities
- workstations and the work environment (including lighting, noise levels, temperature and ventilation, and the physical features of the premises)
- employment arrangements and organisational issues, such as: disability and equality policies; health and safety arrangements and procedures (including risk management and reporting procedures); employment policies and procedures; communications
- organisational culture and attitudes, and related management and staff training

2.15

Help, advice and information can be obtained from the following organisations

(Contact details are provided at the back of this book).

- AbilityNet
- Back Care (The National Organisation for Healthy Backs)
- Employers' Forum on Disability
- The Ergonomic Society
- The Health and Safety Executive (HSE)
- Jobcentre Plus
- The Society of Occupational Medicine

A PRACTICAL GUIDE TO

employment adjustments for people who stammer

Communication tips

Interviews

Reasonable Adjustments

2.16

This guide describes some of the adjustments that can be considered for people who stammer.
The Employers' Forum on Disability gratefully acknowledges the help it has received in preparing this section from the British Stammering Association.

Stammering and the DDA

The Disability Discrimination Act (DDA) 1995 defines a disabled person as someone who has, or had, "a physical or mental impairment, which has a substantial and long-term adverse effect" on their ability to carry out normal day-to-day activities. "Long-term" means that it must have lasted, or be expected to last, at least 12 months.

People who stammer may not consider themselves to be "disabled" but they may well be protected by the DDA definition of disability. Under the Disability Discrimination Act (1995) it is unlawful for an employer to treat a disabled applicant for a job, or an employee, less favourably, without justification.

An employer also has a duty under the DDA to make reasonable adjustments to prevent a disabled employee from being placed at a substantial disadvantage by any physical feature of the premises, or by working arrangements. When deciding whether or not an adjustment is reasonable an employer should consider:

- **the effectiveness of the adjustment in preventing the disadvantage**
- **the practicality of the adjustment**
- **the financial and other costs of the adjustment and the extent of any disruption caused**

- **the extent of the employer's financial or other resources**

- **the availability to the employer of financial or other assistance to help make an adjustment, for example through the Access to Work scheme and the support of the Employment Services' (know as Jobcentre Plus from April 2002) Disability Service Teams**

2.16 It is more prudent to take a positive attitude to attempt to resolve problems and make reasonable adjustments, rather than spend time and money first trying to establish if someone is technically covered by the Act.

What is stammering?

Stammering (also called stuttering) is a speech/fluency difficulty which causes the person to have speech blocks, prolongations, or repetitions of sound. Current research holds that stammering has a physiological basis in the workings of the brain. Stammering does not indicate anything about a person's personality intelligence, competency level or capacity to work at any given level. People who stammer know what they want to say. The difficulty is in the physical production of speech. This can lead to frustration and the person who stammers avoiding certain words or situations. Managers who work with people who stammer need to be sensitive to the person on the one hand, while at the same time exploring what it is about the job that may initially be considered by the person and/or employer to be problematic.

By becoming experienced in making adjustments for people who stammer, your organisation should benefit from better communication generally; many adjustments and etiquette will benefit everyone.

Who is affected?

Almost 1%, or around 500,000, of adults in the UK stammer, with men four times more likely to stammer than women. It is rare to completely lose a stammer; most people stammer to a greater or lesser extent at different times. Stammering can improve within a supportive environment and also through speech therapy.

Each person will stammer differently and the extent of their stammer will vary from day to day.

A person who stammers may have particular difficulties with:

- **interviews**

- **presentations and meetings**

- **tiredness, time pressure or anxiety**

- **using the telephone**

The individual facts should always be considered in consultation with the individual. Assumptions should not be made, such as assuming the person is just nervous or shy. The pressure to speak quickly and the attitude and response of the listener often exacerbate the difficulties listed. Therefore, good communication is vital.

Communication tips

- **listen to the person and allow them to finish what they are saying; do not interrupt and/or attempt to finish their words or sentences. Give the person time to deal with speech blocks (when words are difficult to get out), as this is very helpful**

- **maintain eye contact as much as possible**

- **speak normally in a relaxed manner; if you speak quickly this may increase the person's stammer**

- **allow extra time for communication**

By making adjustments and communicating effectively with people who stammer, your organisation can benefit from highly effective communicators who stammer. People who stammer are more likely, because they know they will have to try harder with the spoken word, to:

- **plan better what they want to say**

- **think before they speak and**

- **get to the point quicker**

Reasonable adjustments – recruitment

Although most people who stammer will be able to carry out most jobs, in some cases it may be necessary to adjust the job specification to avoid discrimination. The key is to decide what is an essential part of the job and what could be done in a different way or reallocated to another member of the team. For example, if the person has difficulties with telephone work, consider whether it is essential or only a small part of the job and whether these duties can be easily allocated to another member of the team. Also consider whether they can communicate with others in an alternative way, for example by email or writing.

People who stammer should not be refused a job or an interview on the grounds that the job requires 'excellent communication skills'. Assumptions should not be made, as people who stammer may well have excellent oral and communication skills. People who stammer have succeeded in many areas, including sales and customer service.

There is no justification for arguing that customers won't like being served by someone who stammers.

Employees who stammer can make a valuable contribution to the workplace as they are likely to be more aware of the need to prepare for meetings and presentations, and of customer needs and communication issues. Focussed listening, clear thinking, approachability and an interest in people are qualities that do not depend on fluent speech.

Interviews

As with most people, a job interview can be the single most difficult speaking situation for someone who stammers. Their stammer may increase, particularly when the person is enthusiastic. As well as being under pressure, like every other applicant, a person who stammers has the added stress created by trying to get their point across while worrying about the interviewer's reactions. The person may unintentionally come across as reticent, hesitant or confused, by pausing before words and/or using words such as "you know", "well actually", and "it could be said".

2.16

Interviewers should focus on what the person says about their experience, abilities and skills. As stammering can vary depending on how the person and listener interact, it may be useful to allow extra time for an interview and to follow the communication tips in this guide.

Be careful if you use telephone interviews, as these may not allow someone who stammers a fair interview. Ask if the applicant is happy with a telephone interview, and be prepared to offer an alternative interview process, for example a face-to-face interview.

In conjunction with an interview, written evidence can also be used as evidence of the person's competencies for the post.

Any concerns about how stammering may affect the person's ability to do the job can be discussed towards the end of the interview. Remember that the interview situation is an artificial and tense environment. Once in post and after a proper induction, the individual is likely to stammer significantly less than in the interview.

Other tests

It is essential that you consider whether the skills tested are necessary for the post or whether any adjustments need to be made to the test. If a stammer increases significantly under stress it may well be appropriate to allow more time for an oral test or allow it to be in a written form. If specific oral skills are required, for example public speaking or customer service, employers should consider the applicant's work history in conjunction with an oral test for evidence of those skills.

Case Study – DfES

An employee for DfES has been working in a role that requires good communication skills. However, although he communicates well in one-to-one situations, his stammer becomes more severe in stressful situations. This has been a problem when he is interviewed for promotion. DfES are reviewing their processes to ensure that at his next interview this is taken into account. DfES talked to the employee about the difficulties he has experienced in past interviews. One problem was that when he was having a speech block, the interviewers asked further questions rather than waiting for him to finish his answer, and assumed that he did not know the answer. DfES are keen to provide information to interviewers before the interview to ensure they know what to do, or not to do, if the interviewee gets blocked – they will be using this briefing guide as part of that process.

Another difficulty was that the employee avoided certain words that he knew he would stammer in the interview. As a result he did not answer some questions as fully as the interviewers were expecting. DfES have worked with the employee to explore other phraseology which would enable him to answer the question fully, but not use a word that he would be likely to stammer.

The employee is keen to show that he can perform well in an interview – he does not want to write everything down as he manages well in one-to-one situations. However, he will be putting together a portfolio of written evidence to demonstrate his competencies for the post which he can produce if he is unable to answer all the questions as fully as he would wish.

Another adjustment will be to allow the interviewee to be interviewed by one panel member at a time instead of by two or three together which should help reduce the likelihood of stammering. A silent observer, out of eyeshot, will ensure fairness.

DfES have discussed all these measures with the employee and will be trying them out with him at an interview shortly.

Harassment

Someone who stammers may be harassed by colleagues who make fun of the person's stammer. The employer is ultimately responsible, in law, for any acts of harassment by employees. If your organisation has a disability and/or equal opportunity policy, you should make clear that any harassment, including on the grounds of disability will not be tolerated and that any offenders will be dealt with through the organisation's disciplinary procedures. Disability awareness and equal opportunity training should help in raising awareness of what is and what isn't acceptable.

Case studies – Leicestershire County Council

Paul works for Leicestershire County Council's Direct Labour Organisation (DLO) and has done for many years in Central Stores. The DLO are responsible for highways maintenance and repair work for the majority of the County. The organisation works in a high-pressured contract working environment.

Staff at DLO support Paul by listening and allowing him plenty of time to speak. If necessary, colleagues repeat his words to make sure they understand what he is saying. Paul performs well and is a valued worker.

2.16

Dean works for a company that manufactures high quality children's footwear. He works as a computer stitch operator, but is also able to carry out a wide range of other operations within the company. At the early stages of employment the Employment Service were involved who recommended support from the Workstep programme, managed contractually by Leicestershire County Council.

Dean has cerebral palsy and stammers. The company has financial support from Workstep so a support worker can work alongside Dean and help Dean with some of his duties. They also access to an Employment Support Worker who advises Dean and the company if difficulties arise. Dean also took the initiative and, with the support of his doctor, was referred to speech therapy classes. This made a real improvement to his stammer and boosted his self-confidence. Dean continues to stammer, but with confidence.

Reasonable adjustments – employment

The same basic etiquette when conversing with someone who stammers should be used when the person is doing the job, i.e. listening to the person and allowing them to finish what they are saying, maintaining eye contact, etc.

You should try not to make assumptions about the skills, abilities and goals of an employee who stammers; they should be given the same opportunities in work as anyone else, including promotion.

Talk to the employee and encourage training and work opportunities in areas that the person may have previously avoided, but for which they could well have excellent skills. For example, the employee may be reluctant to participate in meetings because of their stammer. It may be necessary to help build the person's self-confidence for this task as part of their professional and personal development. Indeed, personal development and performance plans could include goals for improving important communication skills, in agreement with the employee. You could agree on certain tasks that can be monitored, for example, talking at meetings, greeting clients and company visitors, and giving in-house or external presentations. Above all, have an open-door approach to aid good lines of communication. Some further adjustments that you should consider:

Training

- a training course in communication skills or telephone skills for the employee
- sponsoring the employee for a speech course. This often increases fluency and has long-term gains in communication skills and confidence
- disability awareness training that includes stammering, so colleagues know how to best communicate with someone who stammers

Meetings and presentations

- ensure the employee has an opportunity to speak at meetings
- encourage the employee to arrive a few minutes early for meetings. This will enable time to relax and to slow their rate of speech
- allow extra time in face to face meetings
- if the person is to give a presentation, make sure they have the support and preparation they need in order to feel confident about their material

Telephone work

People who stammer usually have more difficulty on the telephone, as information is solely through verbal cues. Adjustments could include:

- allowing extra time, particularly if there are targets for employees to speak to a certain number of clients in a specified time period
- using other forms of communication, for example email or Typetalk (the national relay service which enables deaf, hard of hearing, deafened and speech-impaired people to communicate with hearing people using the telephone network)
- using a script for some key parts of a call
- modifying a script if one is used, for example in a call centre, so the employee can avoid certain words that are particularly difficult

2.16

Other adjustments

- make sure the person has support and preparation time and is confident in undertaking a role
- reallocate minor or subsidiary duties, for example making or answering occasional phone calls
- modify assessments or appraisals in line with any communication difficulties identified and/or being addressed so that someone is not marked down on communication skills in an assessment because they stammer

By investing in the development of employees who stammer you will obviously also gain as the person is able to contribute more to your organisation. You may also benefit from more effective communication across the team as colleagues also learn valuable communication skills. As good communication techniques are shared, you will also learn as an organisation how to better serve customers who don't speak fluently, or, for example whose first language is not English.

2.16

Case Study – Brent Library Service

Christine is a Senior Customer Services Officer for Brent Library Service. She is responsible for a staff of 20 at a library. She also manages a team of Customer Services Officers who manage five other libraries in the area.

Christine has worked for Brent Library Service all her working life, and in the past fifteen years has taken opportunities offered for promotion. She says, "Over the years my line managers have been particularly supportive in suggesting how I could develop my career, and exploit my strengths of communicating with people."

Support she has been given includes being:

- **allowed to write interview answers, for a particularly stressful interview**
- **encouraged to complete a presentation course**
- **responsible for training staff in her area in customer care**
- **allowed paid time off for a speech therapy course**
- **encouraged to take the lead on service-wide disability awareness training**

Although she often uses the telephone, Christine aims to reduce her time on the telephone by using email. She also organises the staffing of the front line service so she is not usually the first point of contact on the telephone. People with good telephone skills answer the telephone and she serves customers face to face, so the team is strengthened.

Help, advice and information can be obtained from the following organisations

(Contact details are provided at the back of this book).

- **BT Textdirect**
- **British Stammering Association**
- **Disability Rights Commission**
- **Employers Forum on Disability**
- **Jobcentre Plus**
- **RNID Typetalk**
- **Royal College of Speech and Language Therapists**

A PRACTICAL GUIDE TO

employment adjustments for people with HIV

- HIV and the DDA
- HIV Policy
- Reasonable adjustments
- Confidentiality
- Travelling and working overseas

2.17

The management of people with HIV should be consistent with policies and procedures developed for people affected by other serious and potentially progressive medical conditions. If adjustments are required, this section should be read in conjunction with Chapter 2.9 'A practical guide to employment adjustments for people with progressive or fluctuating conditions'.

The Employers' Forum on Disability gratefully acknowledges the help it has received in preparing this section from Positive Futures and The National AIDS Trust.

What is HIV?

HIV (Human Immunodeficiency Virus) is a virus that damages the cells of the immune system making it less able to fend off illness. The virus makes copies of itself using the person's own body cells. Shortly after infection, the person may have flu-like symptoms (called 'seroconversion illness') that usually pass. There is then a period of asymptomatic infection where the person has no related illness. This can last many years. If the person becomes ill because their immune system has been compromised by HIV infection, then that person has symptomatic HIV infection.

AIDS (Acquired Immune Deficiency Syndrome), occurs when a number of specific infections or cancers develop as a result of HIV infection. However, largely due to medical advances, this is by no means an inevitable conclusion of HIV infection.

HIV does not grow outside the body. Transmission can only occur when the blood, semen, or vaginal secretions of a person who is HIV positive enters another person's bloodstream. The risk

2.17

of infection is therefore low. This is especially so in the workplace, where there should already be standard procedures covering health and safety (as set out in The Health and Safety Act 1974) and first aid procedures.

According to the Public Health Laboratory Service, fewer people now die from HIV in the UK (in 1996, 1430 people died who had HIV; in 2000 this figure fell to 411). This is largely due to the success of combination therapy, where a combination of drugs slows the replication of the virus and gives the immune system a chance to rebuild itself. It is not a cure, but it does slow or halt the progression of HIV.

For combination therapy to be successful, the person needs to keep to a rigorous schedule of drugs. They may also need to be strict about what and when they eat and drink. There may be unpleasant side-effects as the body takes time to adjust to medication, for example nausea, diarrhoea and headaches. People will react differently and will not have every side-effect. After a few weeks side-effects may disappear, or be managed through different drugs or by altering the dosage.

Some side-effects may last longer, for example changes in body shape or an increased risk of diabetes. After a few years, at least half of those on combination therapy have a surge in viral replication as the drugs stop working. There is then a need to switch to second or third combinations.

Who is affected?

According to the Public Health Laboratory Service, there are at least 33,500 people living with HIV in the UK. More people are diagnosed each year (4,412 in 2000-2001), with an increasing number of heterosexuals being diagnosed. The majority of people who have HIV are people of working age and may well be your customers or clients. You may also:

- **have people with HIV applying for jobs**
- **be managing existing employees who have HIV but currently have no symptoms**
- **be managing the retention of those who are starting long-term treatment, and are able to continue working**
- **have employees who are unaware they have HIV, because they have not been tested**

The Regulatory Environment

HIV and the DDA

Under the Disability Discrimination Act (DDA) (1995), it is unlawful for an employer to unjustifiably treat a disabled applicant for a job, or an employee, less favourably, or to fail to make reasonable adjustments for the disabled person.

The DDA defines a disabled person as someone who has, or had, "a physical or mental impairment, which has a substantial and long-term adverse effect" on their ability to carry out normal day-to-day activities. It also covers recurring and progressive conditions, past impairments, and conditions that would have a substantial adverse effect on the person's normal day-to-day activities, but for controlling treatment or medication. People with HIV who may not consider themselves to be "disabled" may therefore be protected by the DDA, because HIV can be a progressive condition, controlled by drugs.

Progressive conditions

The DDA provides that a person with a progressive condition is "to be regarded as having an impairment which has a substantial adverse effect on his or her ability to carry out normal day-to-day activities before it actually does so. Where a person has such a progressive condition, he or she will be treated as having an impairment which has a substantial adverse effect from the moment any impairment resulting from that condition first has some effect, however slight, on their ability to carry out normal day-to-day activities."

The government plans to alter the definition of disability so that a person with HIV will be covered from the date of diagnosis; they will not have to prove that they have a progressive condition in order to be protected. No date for this change has been set.
An employer has a duty under the DDA to make reasonable adjustments to prevent a disabled employee from being placed at a substantial disadvantage by any physical feature of the premises, or by working arrangements. The duty applies to all aspects of employment, including recruitment and selection, training, transfer, career development and retention. When deciding whether or not an adjustment is reasonable an employer should consider:

- **the effectiveness of the adjustment in preventing the disadvantage**
- **the practicality of the adjustment**
- **the financial and other costs of the adjustment and the extent of any disruption caused**
- **the extent of the employer's financial or other resources**
- **the availability to the employer of financial or other assistance to help make an adjustment, for example through the Access to Work scheme and the support of the Jobcentre Plus' Disability Service Teams**

It is better to take a positive attitude and resolve problems by making reasonable adjustments than spend time and money trying to establish whether or not someone is technically covered by the Act. Taking proactive steps on HIV awareness and policy will enable you to avoid discriminating against people with HIV, to retain good employees, and to avoid disruption, costs and adverse publicity.

Other equal opportunity legislation

HIV can affect people of any race, nationality, gender or sexual orientation. The Race Relations Act and the Sex Discrimination Act already outlaw harassment in the UK on the grounds of race and gender respectively. The UK government is obliged, under the 'EU Directive on Equal Treatment in Employment and Occupation' to bring into force legislation to outlaw discrimination in employment on grounds of sexual orientation, as well as religion and belief by 2003 and age by 2006. The UK already has legislation in the form of the DDA on disability discrimination.

2.17

Case study

Five years ago Daniel was at his lowest ebb – HIV positive and waiting to die. He started treatment which restored his physical health, but he was still depressed and had low self-esteem. To gain confidence and skills, Daniel completed a college course and then arranged to see Positive Futures. After a couple of meetings he was offered an interview for a work placement with Impact, an advertising agency. Daniel was successful and started the placement. "My first day was one of the best days of my life. Everyone was supportive and there for me if I needed help. I fitted in and they didn't need to make any concessions for me, I was just like one of the team". When a vacancy for Marketing Assistant arose, Daniel applied and was offered the job. Since then, he has had a pay rise and his responsibilities have increased. **This example demonstrates that often the only change needed is attitudinal; the employer showed a willingness to give the person a chance; no workplace adjustments were required in this case.**

HIV policy

Most employers want to ensure employees, including those with HIV, are treated fairly, consistently, and without prejudice. Given the widespread fear, stigma and discrimination surrounding HIV, and the fact that HIV is a recruitment, retention, and health issue, organisations should adopt a policy on HIV, or build one into existing policies, for example making it explicitly clear that a disability policy covers HIV.

Your policies can, and should, demonstrate high-level commitment, making it easier to:

- **educate employees about the transmission of HIV and explain the actual risk of HIV in the workplace**
- **clarify or define employee responsibilities, for example to respect their colleague's right to keep their HIV status confidential**
- **stress that harassment of anyone with HIV will not be tolerated and**

that disciplinary action will always be taken against anyone found to be harassing an employee or customer with HIV

- **describe the organisation's responsibilities and provide guidelines for managers on, for example, how to make reasonable adjustments under the Disability Discrimination Act, and how to ensure good communication whilst respecting confidentiality (management development courses that connect to these issues should also be highlighted)**
- **outline the level of support and flexibility that may be available without someone with HIV having to disclose their status**
- **help to change deeply felt fears or prejudices, often caused by a lack of knowledge, for example the assumption that HIV only affects certain groups**
- **engender confidence in employees that the organisation takes HIV and it's responsibilities seriously**
- **help to ensure fair and consistent behaviour towards everyone**
- **place HIV in the context of other relevant policies**
- **demonstrate your commitment to being a fair employer**

Your organisation could take part in World Aids Day (December 1st each year), to educate your employees and provide a focal point for the dissemination of information. Contact the National AIDS Trust for more details.

Multi-national organisations

For organisations that have employees in countries where HIV is widespread, the business case for best practice on HIV may be even stronger as a sizeable number of your employees may have HIV. It also demonstrates corporate social responsibility. You will need to have a separate HIV policy and respond to the economic impact and the welfare of employees in certain countries. You may want to consider partnerships with local governments and educating employees about the risks and transmission of HIV. As your organisation builds its knowledge on HIV in one country, you will be able to use this learning for the benefit of your business worldwide. For more information on developing global policy, contact the Global Business Coalition on HIV/AIDS and the ILO.

2.17

Disclosure

As a person's HIV status is not obvious, the employer must rely on the employee to disclose. Employees are often reluctant to do this, because they fear discrimination, and feel it is not relevant to their ability to do the job. If applicants know that you have a positive equal opportunity policy, and in

2.17

particular that there is a willingness to make reasonable adjustments for all disabled applicants and employees, they will be much more inclined to disclose any disability, including HIV. Disclosure can be beneficial because:

- **the stress of not divulging a disability can exacerbate the person's difficulties at work**
- **the employee and their manager can then determine together what adjustments, if any would maintain or improve performance**
- **the support of fellow workers can be enlisted**

Confidentiality

Under the Data Protection Act, you need to safeguard the confidentiality of an applicant or employee's personal and medical information. When a person's HIV status is known, you should avoid unnecessary and damaging disclosures – disclosure should only occur when:

- **absolutely necessary**
- **with the explicit consent of the individual**
- **it helps to facilitate the person's ability to do the job**

In some cases, a breach of confidentiality by an employer may be unlawful under the DDA.

You should record medical and personal information in a way that does not render it vulnerable. Under the Data Protection Act, the applicant or employee should know who will have access to this information and have agreed to this in writing. Remember that, for anyone with any disability, including HIV:

- **when an employee has told, for example a member of the human resources department, their line manager, or occupational health department about the disability, in confidence, the employer is deemed under the DDA to know that the person is disabled. It is therefore essential to train staff onhow to deal with such disclosures and any accompanying need for reasonable adjustments**
- **if an adjustment is necessary, (for example, time off work, or non standard hours) the employee's line manager will need to know the adjustment is required but neither they nor colleagues need to be told the precise medical reasons**

Harassment

Many people with HIV experience harassment, often serious harassment, at work. You are ultimately responsible, under the DDA, to take all reasonable steps to deal with harassment.

You should make clear that any harassment, including on the grounds of disability, will not be tolerated and that offenders will be dealt with through the organisation's disciplinary procedures. You should also make it clear that refusal to work with people because they have HIV is unacceptable and will not be tolerated.

Disability awareness and equal opportunity training should help in raising awareness of what is and what isn't acceptable. People tend to make assumptions about lifestyle and HIV. Awareness of HIV should include the fact that anyone can become infected with HIV.

First aid

Given that you will not know every employee who has HIV, safe first aid practices should always be implemented.

Misconceptions surround first aid and HIV. All first aid training covers HIV/AIDS as one of the blood borne infections. Training should teach first aiders to cover their own open wounds before treating anyone who is bleeding. The first aider should be aware of the necessary equipment, such as gloves and mouth-to-mouth resuscitation aids. These can be ordered from whoever supplies your first aid equipment. However, it is important to stress that the chances of contracting HIV through first aid procedures are very slim: no one has so far been infected by giving someone first aid.

Reasonable adjustments – recruitment

You need to ensure that you do not discriminate against someone with HIV during the recruitment procedure. You may also have to make reasonable adjustments to the recruitment procedure. It is unnecessary and potentially discriminatory (under the DDA) to ask someone about their HIV status on application forms or at interview, if adverse decisions are made as a result, unless these can be justified. Likewise, pre or post employment screening for HIV may be discriminatory under the Disability Discrimination Act if this leads to a job offer being unjustifiably withdrawn or altered. The risk of infection of HIV is extremely low in the workplace, and good standards of health and safety should render the risk negligible. Nearly all risks can be handled with appropriate precautions.

Adjustments may need to be made to the shortlisting process, because an applicant may:

- **apply for a job for which they are over qualified because they need to regain confidence**
- **have gaps in their c.v. due to illness**
- **have done voluntary work**

Adjustments for people with HIV will depend on the person's medication and/or any illnesses caused by a weaker immune system. Always check with the individual what adjustments are needed. Adjustments are often simple and would be best practice for all applicants. These include:

- **flexibility around times and dates**
- **building in rest or toilet breaks**
- **providing ready access to drinking water**

2.17

Akkerman v City Centre Restaurants (UK) Ltd

Mr Akkermann, who was HIV positive, started his employment with City Centre Restaurants in June 1997 and transferred to a different branch in October. He was ill in his second week and complained about excessively long shifts. No action was taken. He was ill again in early December and subsequently resigned. During the tribunal, a medical report showed that 'it is quite possible that if his timetable had been reduced he may have been able to continue his work'. The tribunal noted that even if the shift pattern had been altered, he may not have found the long hours and physical demands of the job easy. However, Mr Akkermann might have been able to work part-time, if adjustments had been made; there was no evidence that he would have been dismissed on grounds of conduct or capability. He was awarded £20,807.58, including £5,000 for injury to feelings and £9,939.20 for loss of earnings.

Reasonable adjustments – employment

The key to managing any employee – including one with HIV – is good communication. You must ensure that confidentiality is respected. Most people with HIV will not need any adjustments, apart from time off for clinic appointments to monitor and maintain their health. If adjustments are required they are usually as a result of side-effects of treatment. They do not usually seriously inhibit work performance, but may cause temporary inconvenience for the individual.

Whether an employee with HIV is returning to work or starting work you should ensure they have a thorough induction period. It may be beneficial to provide peer support or career counselling to build confidence and skills.

Be prepared to review adjustments should HIV related illnesses arise and then consider reallocating duties. Adjustments will depend on the nature of the HIV related illness and the treatment. This book gives many examples of specific impairments and workplace adjustments. Types of adjustments include allowing ad hoc toilet breaks or allowing the person to work from home if the person has diarrhoea (usually a short term adjustment due to a change in drug treatment) or flexible working hours or short breaks if the person has fatigue. Other simple adjustments include an ergonomic assessment of seating arrangements if the person's weight loss leads to discomfort (sometimes only a cushion is needed), or screen magnification or screen reading software if the person has a visual impairment.

If an employee is undergoing drug treatment, they may need a significant number of pills and to be strict about what and when they eat. You should:

- **ensure drinking water is readily available**
- **provide easy access to food/food preparation areas wherever possible and be flexible over eating times**
- **give the employee notice of any disruption to routine, for example canteen closure, training days, or overtime and travel requirements**
- **ensure the employee can store medication safely and confidentially**
- **allow the employee flexibility to attend clinic appointments when necessary**

Time off for rehabilitation, treatment and HIV related illness

Rehabilitation

Do not assume that employees with HIV will take a lot of time off sick. They may need the occasional clinic appointment to monitor and maintain their health. Appointments are:

- **usually every 3 months**
- **usually carried out by NHS clinics so the appointments are likely to be in working hours**
- **likely to be infrequent but regular so they can be planned in advance**

They should not pose any more difficulties than similar arrangements you probably already manage, such as doctor or dentist appointments or arrangements with other specialists. Time off for rehabilitation and treatment is a reasonable adjustment under the DDA for a disabled person.

Treatment

The first few months of treatment are often the most difficult and the employee may have to travel further to a more specialist centre. They may need to attend a clinic more frequently to ensure any treatment failure is spotted and the treatment changed accordingly. If treatment failure occurs, or there is a change to a new drug, some people may experience some psychological difficulties. The employer should ensure they are supportive and look at short-term adjustments, such as reallocating tasks and extending deadlines. With new treatment, it may take a few weeks for side-effects to settle down.

2.17

HIV related absence

Some people may need short periods of time off due to bouts of illness. Absences should be managed according to the standards outlined in Chapter 1.5 'A practical guide to managing sickness absence'. You should discuss with the employee whether or not they want their HIV status to remain confidential. Only Human Resources or Occupational Health need to know the cause of absences. Self-certificated absences for HIV related absences should refer to the specific illness and not the fact that it is HIV related.

Pensions and benefits

It is unlawful under the DDA to have a blanket ban on disabled people joining an occupational pension scheme. It is however permissible to exclude a disabled employee from the scheme if the costs of providing benefits would be substantially greater than for a non-disabled employee. The employer would need actuarial advice and/or medical evidence in each case to justify such exclusion.

The duty of reasonable adjustment does not apply to the provision of benefits under an occupational pension scheme. However, best practice should allow everyone to take advantage of these benefits by considering:

- **how the scheme can be adapted to provide every employee, including those with progressive/fluctuating conditions, with the same benefits, or**
- **what alternative provision can be made for people with such conditions**

Insurance

The DDA makes broadly similar provisions for group insurance schemes as for occupational pension schemes. Best practice should allow everyone to enjoy the same insurance benefits as everyone else. Consider:

- **insurance companies that cover people with particular disabilities**
- **if you cannot find alternative cover, offer other benefits of a similar value**
- **if the insurer wishes to reassess future premiums in light of any claims they should be asked to justify this with actuarial evidence. You can point out that claims concerning HIV are rare and that your organisation believes continuing to provide this benefit is a priority**

Healthcare work settings

If the employer is a healthcare organisation, you should keep abreast of the Department of Health's guidance for health care workers with HIV, professional regulatory bodies' statements of ethical responsibilities and occupational health guidelines. Healthcare workers should know their rights and responsibilities; all professional regulatory bodies have statements detailing members ethical responsibilities covering HIV and emphasising the duty of care owed by health workers to patients. Precautions will also help protect employees from infection from patients who have HIV, although it should be noted that the risk of infection in a healthcare setting is very low.

Appropriate training should be given to everyone who comes into contact with bodily fluids and/or needles and sharp instruments to prevent injuries and the risk of infection, including HIV infection.

In certain healthcare settings an employee's HIV status may need to be disclosed to their colleagues. If this is necessary, the employer should discuss with the employee how best to do this.

Case study

Employers need to ensure that managers, through training and development, feel confident about managing disabled employees, including those with HIV.

Guy's and St Thomas' Trust run a one day course, 'What every manager should know about HIV'. Targeted at personnel, operational, clinical or directorate managers, occupational health staff, or others with management responsibility the day gives delegates:

- **accurate and current information on HIV, including epidemiology, transmission and course of infection**
- **pertinent details of employment legislation**
- **good working practices in relation to the employment and management of people with HIV and AIDS**
- **knowledge of the department of health guidelines on the employment and management of HIV positive healthcare workers**
- **procedures for managing an occupational exposure to HIV**

They also run a 'HIV Study Day for Occupational Health Practioners' where there is an opportunity to practice the knowledge and skills gained with reference to occupational health settings.

2.17

Travelling and working overseas

If your employees are required to travel abroad, you should provide information on risks associated with such travel, including advice on sexual transmission, HIV, and the reliability of blood products abroad. The Department of Health's 'Health advice for travellers' and 'Travel Safe – advice for travellers on avoiding the risks of HIV and AIDS' should be circulated. This will also help inform people with HIV who may not be able to travel because they cannot take the necessary vaccines, or who may have to arrange specialised travel insurance to cover HIV related illnesses or treatment. Contact the National AIDS

2.17

Trust for details of travel insurance that covers people with HIV. You may also want to allow employees to arrange their own travel insurance, and reimburse them, rather than use group travel insurance. This enables employees with certain medical statuses, including HIV, to obtain insurance without necessarily having to disclose their medical information.

Some countries require evidence that travellers do not have HIV before a visa or work permit can be issued. This should be brought to the attention of any employee who is due to work overseas.

If a work permit or visa cannot be obtained because of the person's HIV status, consider other countries where there are no visa restrictions. If a core part of the person's job is to travel to countries where a visa cannot be obtained then you may need to consider redeployment. These decisions need to be made in consultation with the employee; it must be stressed **do not to base such decisions on management assumptions.**

Help advice and information can be obtained from the following organisations

(Contact details are provided at the back of this book).

- **Department of Health**
- **Employers Forum on Disability**
- **Global Business Coalition on HIV/AIDS**
- **ILO**
- **Jobcentre Plus**
- **National AIDS Trust**
- **Positive futures**
- **Terrence Higgins Trust**
- **www.aidsmap.com**

Help and Information

Employers' Forum on Disability
Nutmeg House, 60 Gainsford Street
London, SE1 2NY
Tel: 020 7403 3020
Text: 020 7403 0040
Fax: 020 7403 0404
Email: efd@employers-forum.co.uk
Website: www.employers-forum.co.uk
Information line provides business advice and guidance on disability in the workplace and regarding disabled customers.

in alphabetical order

AbilityNet
PO Box 94, Warwick CV34 5WS
Tel/text: 01926 312 847
Freephone: 0800 269 545
Fax: 01926 407 425
Email: Enquiries@AbilityNet.co.uk
Website: www.abilitynet.co.uk
Advice about adaptive computer technology. Carry out assessments for computer users and suggest solutions. Two open days each month to view specialist equipment.

ACAS (The Advisory, Conciliation and Arbitration Service)
Can help with factual information on the legislation and assistance related to its effects on industrial relations practices and procedures. ACAS has a duty to offer conciliation in complaints of discrimination to industrial tribunals. ACAS offices are in the telephone book under 'ACAS'.

Adult Dyslexia Organisation
336 Brixton Road, London SW9 7AA
Helpline: 020 7924 9559
Office: 020 7737 7646
Fax: 020 7207 7796
Email: dyslexia.hq@dial.pipex.com
Website: www.futurenet.co.uk/charity/ado
Offers advice about psychological and teacher assessments, tuition, a helpline, a research group, a Newsletter and various pamphlets and videos.

Adult Dyslexia and Skills Development Centre
5 Tavistock Place, London WC1H 9SN
Tel: 020 7388 8744
Fax: 020 7387 7968
Email: dyslexia@adsdc.freeserve.co.uk
The Centre offers psychological diagnostic assessment and/or counselling, tuition and training, advocacy and awareness raising through telephone advice, lectures, talks and workshops and publications.

Back Care (The National Organisation for Healthy Backs)
16 Elmtree Road, Teddington, Middlesex TW11 8ST
Tel: 020 8977 5474
Fax: 01926 407 425
Email: website@backcare.org.uk
Website: www.backpain.org

BT Textdirect
BT Textdirect enables deaf, deafblind, deafened, hard of hearing and speech-impaired people to communicate with each other and hearing people. Most people can use BT TextDirect to make a call. To make a call, dial one of the following prefixes:
Text users: 18001
Voice users: 18002
followed by the full telephone number of the person you wish to call.
An operator is brought into the call automatically if this is required.

British Deaf Association
1-3 Worship Street, London EC2A 2AB
Tel: 020 7588 3520
Text: 020 7588 3529
Fax: 020 7588 3527
Videophone: 020 7496 9539
Email: helpline@bda.org.uk
Website: www.bda.org.uk
National organisation of deaf people. Produce British Deaf News.

British Dyslexia Association
98 London Road, Reading RG1 5AU
Helpline: 0118 9668271
Admin: 0118 9662677
Fax: 0118 9351927
Email: info@dyslexiahelpbda.demon.co.uk
Website: www.bda-dyslexia.org.uk
Provides a support network, helpline, computer advice service, publications, teacher training, conferences and exhibitions.

British Epilepsy Association
New Anstey House, Gate Way Drive, Yeadon, Leeds LS19 7XY
Tel: 0808 800 5050
Fax: 0808 800 5555
Email: helpline@bea.org.uk
Website: www.epilepsy.org.uk
Provides information and support on epilepsy, restricted occupations, and first aid.

British Stammering Association
15 Old Ford Road, London E2 9PJ
Tel: 020 8983 1003
Fax: 020 8983 3591
Email: mail@stammering.org
Website: www.stammering.org
Information and advice on stammering for people who stammer and employers.

Centre for Accessible Environments
Nutmeg House, 60 Gainsford Street
London, SE1 2NY
Tel & Minicom:020 7357 8182
Fax: 020 7357 8183
Email: cae@globalnet.co.uk
Has produced a comprehensive, step by step guide to setting up Personal Escape Plans for disabled people called; "Personal Emergency Egress Plans". Provides information and advice on access issues and part M of the Building Regulations; training and consultancy on legislation; factsheets and publications including an access audit pack for appraising the accessibility of buildings for disabled users. Carries out access audits.

The Council for Advancement of Communication with Deaf People (CACDP)
Durham University Science Park
Block 4, Stockton Road, Durham
DH1 3UZ
Tel/Text: 0191 383 1155
(voice and minicom)
Text only: 0191 383 7915
Fax: 0191 383 7914
Email: durham@cacdp.org.uk
Website: www.cacdp.org.uk
Produces a national directory of qualified sign language interpreters and lipspeakers, classified by region, experience and expertise.

DVLA
DVLC, Swansea, SA6 7JL
Customer Enquiries: 0870 240 0009
Fax: 01792 783 071
Text: 01792 782 787
Website: www.dvla.gov.uk
Provides information on driving requirements and epilepsy.

Davies Associates
Glebe House, Llanharry
Glamorgan CF72 9LH
Tel & Fax: 01443 226 216
Email: Davies@glebel.demon.co.uk
Employment Medico-Legal Specialists
Consultancy advice on occupational Health and Safety practice for employers, doctors, lawyers and disability interest groups. Good practice guidance; tribunal reviews/ commentary; case commissions.

Department of Health
Richmond House, 79 Whitehall,
London SW1A 2NS
Tel: 020 7210 4850
Text: 020 7210 5025
Email: dhmail@doh.gsi.gov.uk
Website: www.doh.gov.uk
Produces 'Health advice for travellers' and Travel Safe: advice for travellers on avoiding the risks of HIV and AIDS (National Aids Helpline 0800 567 123).

Diabetes UK
(formerly British Diabetic Association)
10 Parkway, London NW1 7AA
Tel: 020 7424 1000
Fax: 020 7424 1001
Email: careline@diabetes.org.uk
Website: www.diabetes.org.uk
Provides information and support.

Disability Rights Commission
DRC Helpline, FREEPOST MIDO 2164
Stratford-upon-Avon, CV37 9BR
Tel: 08457 622 633
Text: 08457 622 644
Email: ddahelp@stra.sitel.co.uk
Website: www.drc-gb.org

Dyslexia Institute
Headquarters, 133 Gresham Road,
Staines, Middlesex TW18 2AJ
Tel: 01784 463851
Fax: 01784 460747
Email: info@dyslexia-inst.org.uk
Website: www.dyslexia-inst.org.uk
Offers psychological assessments, and tuition support to those assessed by the Institute.

Employers' Forum on Disability
Nutmeg House, 60 Gainsford Street
London, SE1 2NY
Tel: 020 7403 3020
Text: 020 7403 0040
Fax: 020 7403 0404
Email: efd@employers-forum.co.uk
Website: www.employers-forum.co.uk
Information line provides business advice and guidance on disability in the workplace and regarding disabled customers.

The Ergonomics Society
Devonshire Square,
Loughborough LE11 3DW
Tel: 01509 234 904
Fax: 01509 235 666
Email: ergsoc@ergonomics.org.uk
Website: www.ergonomics.org.uk/
Has a list of registered consultants.

Global Business Coalition on HIV/AIDS
1515 Broadway, 45th Floor,
c/o Viacom, New York, NY 10036, USA
Tel: +1 212 846 5893
Fax: +1 212.846 1939
Email: Info@businessfightsaids.org
Website: www.businessfightsaids.org/
A coalition of international businesses dedicated to combating the AIDS epidemic through the business sector's unique skills and expertise

The Health and Safety Executive (HSE)
Rose Court, 2, Southwark Bridge,
London SE1
Tel: 020 7717 6000
Fax: 020 7717 6717
Email: hseinformationservices@natbrit.com
Website: www.hse.gov.uk
The statutory body responsible for ensuring health and safety in the workplace. Advises on prevention, responsibility for inspection and enforcement and good practice.

Her Majesty's Stationary Office
The Stationery Office, PO Box 29
St Crispins House, Duke Street
Norwich NR3 1PD
Tel: 0870 600 5522
Fax: 0870 600 5533
Email: customer.services@tso.co.uk
Website: www.hmso.gov.uk
You can obtain the 'Code of Practice for the elimination of discrimination in the field of employment against disabled persons or persons who have had a disability' from the stationary office.

ILO
4 Route de Morillons,
Ch –1211 Geneva 22, Switzerland
Tel: +41 22 799 6486
Fax: +41 22 799 6349
Email: ILOAIDS@ilo.org.uk
Website: www.ilo.org
Has an international programme on HIV/AIDS and the World of Work and produces a code of practice.

I.R.F.D. (International Register of Firefighters with Diabetes)
Tim Hoy - Secretary
8 Donnington Road, Willesden
London NW10 3QN
Tel: 020 8451 1418
Email: irfduk@globalnet.co.uk
Website: www.welcome.to/irfduk
Provides information and support about discrimination in employment.

Jobcentre Plus:
Disability Service Teams
The Disability Employment Adviser (DEA), as part of the Disability Services Team (DST), gives help and advice on employing and retaining disabled people. The DST also co-ordinates the government's Access to Work programme which provides financial assistance towards the possible extra costs of employing someone with a disability. The DEA or DST can be contacted through your local Jobcentre.

The Long-Term Medical Conditions Alliance
Unit 212, 16 Baldwins Gardens ,
London, EC1N 7RJ
Tel: 020 7813 3637
Fax: 020 7813 3640
Email: alliance@lmca.org.uk
Website: www.lmca.org.uk

The Manic Depression Fellowship
Castle Works, 21 St George's Road,
London SE1 6ES.
Tel: 0207 793 2600.
Fax: 0207 793 2639.
Email: mdf@mdf.org.uk.
Website: www.mdf.org.uk
Provides advice and information on employment issues.

Mind
15-19 Broadway, London E15 4BQ.
Mind InfoLine London: 020 8522 1728.
Outside London: 0345 660 163.
Office Tel: 0208 519 2122.
Fax: 0208 522 1725.
Email: contact@mind.org.uk.
Website: www.mind.org.uk
Works on behalf of people diagnosed, treated or labelled as 'mentally ill'. It has 30 small employment projects.

National AIDS Trust
New City Cloisters, 196 Old Street,
London EC1V 9FR
Tel: 020 7814 6767
Fax: 020 7216 0111
Email: info@nat.org.uk
Website: www.nat.org.uk
Policy and advocacy organisation working to ensure that people in power take action on HIV both within the UK and internationally. Co-ordinates World AIDS day in the UK. Has information on travel insurance that covers people living with HIV.

National Clubhouse Association
Horizon House, 26 Landon Road,
Bromley, Kent, BR2 9JS
Tel: 020 8466 0021
Fax: 020 846 0028.
Email: horizonclubhouse@bun.com
Website: www.clubhouse.uk.org
Clubhouses help people with severe or enduring mental health problems get into employment. They arrange placements with local employers and provide both member and employer with support.

The National Society for Epilepsy
Chesham Lane, Chalfont St Peter
Buckinghamshire SL9 0RJ, England
Tel: 01494 601 300
Fax: 01494 601 337
Helpline: 01494 601 400
Website: www.epilepsynse.org.uk/
Provides information, training and support in medical services and facts on epilepsy.

Positive futures
250 Kennington Lane
London SE11 5RD
Tel: 020 7564 2188
Fax: 020 7564 2140
Email: PFenquiries@ukcoalition.org
Website: www.positive-futures.org/
A partnership of five HIV charities, Terrence Higgins Lighthouse, Chalk Farm Oasis, The Globe Centre, Positively Women and UK Coalition. Advice and consultancy services provide information and guidance on any issues relating to HIV within the workplace. Runs seminars and can also provide bespoke training packages. Organises work placements for people living with HIV, and for supportive employers who want to provide opportunities.

RADAR (Royal Association for Disability And Rehabilitation)
Tel: 020 7250 3222
Minicom: 020 7250 4117
Fax: 020 7250 0212
RADAR has an extensive database and provide information and advice on many of the areas that affect disabled people on a daily basis.

Royal College of Speech and Language Therapists
2/3 White Hart Yard
London, SE1 1NX
Tel: 020 7378 1200
Fax 020 7403 7254
Website: www.rcslt.org
Produces a list of registered speech and language therapists.

The Royal National Institute for the Blind (RNIB)

105 Judd Street, London , WC1H 9NE

Tel: 020 7388 1266

Fax: 020 7388 2034

Helpline: 0845 766 9999

Email: helpline@rnib.org.uk

Website: www.rnib.org.uk/employment

Have a range of employment related services and publications for employers and visually impaired individuals. Publications include information sheets for employers which may be accessed at RNIB's website, the 'Get Back!' series on retention and a free video – 'Ways to Work'.

Royal National Institute for the Blind (RNIB)

224 Great Portland Street, London W1N 6AA

Tel: 020 7388 1266

Fax: 020 7388 2034

Email: informationline@rnid.org.uk

Website: www.rnid.org.uk

Publications include a series of booklets, from the Get Back! Series designed to support newly disabled, injured or long-term sick employees, their employers and vocational rehabilitation professionals in the process of assessment and case-management to help employees remain in work.

The Royal National Institute for Deaf People (RNID)

19-23 Featherstone Street, London EC1Y 8SL

Tel: 0808 808 0123

Text: 0808 808 9000

Fax: 020 7296 8199

Email: informationline@rnid.org.uk

Website: www.rnid.org.uk

RNID Typetalk

PO Box 284, Liverpool, L69 3UZ

0800 959598 (text users)

0800 515152 (voice users)

Email: helpline@rnid-typetalk.org.uk

Typetalk is the national telephone relay service which enables deaf, deafblind, deafened, hard of hearing and speech-impaired people to communicate with hearing people via operators. After calling one of the 0800 numbers, you will be connected to an operator.

RSI Association

380-384 Harrow Road, London W9 2HU

Tel: 020 7266 2000

Helpline: 0800 018 5012

Email: rsia@rsi.org.uk

Website: www.rsi.org.uk

A registered charity providing help and information to people with Repetitive Strain Injury.

Saville and Holdsworth,
The Pavillion, 1 Atwell Place
Thames Ditton, Surrey KT7 0NE.
Helpline: 020 8339 2222.
Email: uk@shlgroup.com.
Website: www.shlgroup.com/direct
Occupational psychologists specialising in testing disabled people as part of the recruitment process, have produced 'Guidelines For Testing People with Disabilities'.

Scottish Association for Mental Health
Information Centre, SAMH, Cumbrae House,
15 Carlton Court, Glasgow, G5 9JP.
Tel: 0141 568 7000.
Fax: 0141 568 7001.
Email: enquire@samh.org.uk.
Website: www.samh.org.uk
Provides a supported employment scheme.

Shaw Trust Information Resource (STIR)
Shaw House, Epsom Square, White Horse Business Park, Trowbridge, Wilts BA14 OXJ.
Tel: 01225 716 350.
Fax: 01225 716 334.
Textphone: 0345 697 288.
Email: stir@shaw-trust.org.uk.
Website: www.shaw-trust.org.uk/
Provides rehabilitation, training, work tasters, employment support. It also supports and advises employers in the employment of people with a disability, including those with mental health problems.

The Society of Occupational Medicine
6 St Andrew's Place, Regent's Park
London NW1 4LB
Tel: 020 7486 2641
Fax: 020 7486 0028
Email:som@sococcmed.demon.co.uk
Website: wwww.som.org.uk
The Society of Occupational Medicine provides details of occupational health physicians. Lists are issued by regional health authority area at £100 each. A regional list contains details on between 50 to 120 occupational health specialists. Information includes contact details, qualifications held, work experience and an explanation of the significance of qualifications. Training and qualifications are conducted by the Faculty of Occupational Medicine at the Royal College of Physicians.

Terrence Higgins Trust
52 - 54 Gray's Inn Road,
London WC1X 8JU
Tel: 020 7831 0330
Fax: 020 7242 0121
Email: info@tht.org.uk
Website: www.tht.org.uk/advice.htm
Have a range of specialist advisers offering free legal advice to anyone affected by HIV & AIDS. Also run regional offices.

www.aidsmap.com
Community-based information based in the UK providing up-to-date information. Has listings of local agencies and produces publications.

Also available from The Employers' Forum on Disability

Recruitment That Works

The guide is based on Centrica's experiences of a New Deal for Disabled People project at their British Gas Trading and Services customer service centres in the North West of England, which led to jobs for 50 disabled people and carers.

Recruitment That Works Sets out step by step instructions for both employers wanting to recruit a diverse workforce and for those agencies that help disadvantaged people into work.

Member price	£15 per copy
Non-member price	£20 per copy

Unlocking Potential

Unlocking Potential presents a case for organisations to learn directly from disabled people. It argues that managing a diverse workforce is increasingly recognised as a key factor in improving efficiency, productivity and overall business sussess. Knowledge of this growing sector of the market, combined with enhanced morale, provides tangible benefits for organisations who are good employers of disabled people.

Promoting Change

This new booklet is designed to assist those involved in promoting or implementing change, commissioning related training or co-ordinating communications on disability. The perfect tool for disability champions, this publication will outline what champions, specific individuals and organisations need to know and do to become disability confident.

Unlocking the Evidence

'Unlocking the Evidence' presents compelling proof that employing disabled people can bring both operational and longer-term strategic business gains, particulary in the light of changing demographics and the new economy.

This book reflects the experience of the UK and international business communities, as well as the latest findings from academic research. 'Unlocking the Evidence' proposes a sophisticated business argument and ends with a call to action – a reminder to the key stakeholders that business, government and the not-for-profit sector must combine forces if business is to benefit fully from diversity and the positive contribution of disabled people.

Videos

The Bigger Picture

Contains excerpts from TV, cinema, performance art and advertisments challenging preconceptions of disabled people. Price £50 per copy

"I use this excellent video to conclude disability seminars and leave people with a positive attitude to the diversity, strength and skills of disabled people"

Phil Friend, Churchill & Friend

Independence 2000

This documentary-style video captures the excitement, humour and the key messages from the Forums' national event in July 2000 – the largest ever gathering of employers, disabled people and major stakeholders around the issue of disability.

Member price	£ 20 per copy
Non-member price	£ 25 per copy

Should you require a any further information, please do not hesitate to contact the publications department on 020 7403 3020 or e-mail publications@employers-forum.co.uk

Index